Birth Order Roles & Sibling Patterns in Individual & Family Therapy

Margaret H. Hoopes, Ph.D.

James M. Harper, Ph.D.

Brigham Young University
Provo, Utah

An Aspen Publication®
Aspen Publishers, Inc.
Rockville, Maryland
Royal Tunbridge Wells
1987

Library of Congress Cataloging-in-Publication Data

Hoopes, Margaret H.
Birth order and sibling patterns in individual and
family therapy.

"An Aspen Publication."
Includes bibliographies and index.
1. Birth order—Psychological aspects. 2. Brothers
and sisters. 3. Psychotherapy. 4. Family psychotherapy.
I. Harper, James M. II. Title [DNLM: 1. Birth Order.
2. Family Therapy. 3. Marital Therapy. 4. Models,
Psychological. 5. Psychotherapy. 6 Sibling Relations.
WM 420 H788b]
RC489.B57H66   1987   616.89   86-31264
ISBN: 0-87189-628-1

Editorial Services: Jane Coyle

Library of Congress Catalog Card Number: 86-32164
ISBN: 0-87189-628-1

Printed in the United States of America

2   3   4   5

Table of Contents

Foreword

The model of family ordinal position presented in this book had its birth in a late night conversation about teaching students to identify family "rules." Jerry Bach and I were attempting to "tease out" the various family systems represented in a couples' therapy group. There seemed to be similarities between certain group members that cut across the family systems and were not accounted for by the family rules. The common factor appeared to be birth order.

During the next several years, we observed hundreds of families and spent thousands of hours watching videotapes of family sessions, listening to audiotapes of family sessions, and talking with each other and with colleagues (including Drs. Hoopes and Harper) in an effort to systematize our observations regarding birth order and its interplay with family rule systems. Gradually, some patterns evolved and some general principles were developed. These principles were tested and refined through further clinical observations. Eventually, we had a primitive model that we could use to conduct seminars about our findings, to draw tentative conclusions, and to develop applications for teaching and therapy.

Drs. Hoopes and Harper have taken that primitive model and refined it. Now the model fairly easily generates testable hypotheses that can further refine it and produce additional information. This book is written primarily to the practitioner; however, it provides down-to-earth, practical principles that will help practitioners understand human behavior and determine appropriate interventions in the home, in the classroom, and particularly in the clinical setting.

Birth order roles do not result from some magical or fatalistic formula, but from factors that are fairly predictable in the systemic development of the family. The roles are taught primarily by parents within the context of the family system and according to the "rules" by which the family system is governed. Hence, although birth order is a major factor in determining the role each child will play, the manner in which the role is played out is determined largely by the family rule system.

Overlaying family systems theory on the birth order model quickly leads the therapist to possible diagnoses, strategic hunches, and therapeutic interventions that would normally take an enormous amount of time. Thus, this book is an invaluable guide to the therapeutic process, be it individual, group, couple, or family therapy. There is no other book quite like it on the market, and I believe it makes a unique contribution to the field of counseling and psychotherapy.

I express my gratitude to Drs. Hoopes and Harper for patiently, thoroughly, and creatively developing our primitive model to the stage reflected by this book and making it available to our profession. I know it has been a labor of love on their part. They have faithfully retained the basic integrity and flavor of our original work, which is a tribute to their own integrity and scholarship.

Alan R. Anderson, Ph.D.

Preface

The existence of a sibling position effect has long been the subject of controversy among behavioral scientists. Birth order research and conceptualization of ideas have been criticized because differences between parents, sibling positions of parents, size of family, and socioeconomic statistics and cultural variables have seldom been taken into account. Because the literature on birth order lacked a coherent theory, applications to therapy seemed intuitive and mystical. Conclusions drawn from research studies on sibling position were often contradictory. We, too, were once skeptical. In the mid-1970s, however, we were introduced to the idea of four basic sibling positions at the Bach Institute in Minneapolis, Minnesota. Based on their clinical observations, interventions in therapy, consultations with many school teachers, and hundreds of hours of discussion, Jerome Bach and Alan Anderson gradually developed complex concepts about the first four sibling positions. They included hypotheses about the way in which the family influences each child; and conversely, the way in which each child influences and serves the family.

We studied the original conceptualizations of Bach and Anderson, and reviewed typed scripts of their conversations about the patterns. We questioned them and discussed their conclusions with them. In addition, we listened to them lecture classes, heard them apply the concepts when they supervised therapists, observed them as they applied the concepts in therapy themselves, participated with them in cotherapy, and received supervision from them. We are indebted to them not only for their ideas, but also for their encouragement to carry their ideas further.

Our experiences with Anderson and Bach launched us into nine years of observing thousands of families, using treatment strategies enlarged by concepts about sibling positions, teaching the concepts in classes and workshops, and receiving feedback from individuals regarding their family experiences. As a result, we integrated all descriptions of sibling positions into characteristic patterns of responses. We developed descriptions of marital and parent-child combinations and formulated guidelines for therapists and supervisors. These activities led to the development of the systems approach to four sibling positions discussed in this book. Although originally influenced by Bach and Anderson, our descriptions of sibling positions represent the evolution of our concepts and beliefs.

Birth Order Roles and Sibling Patterns in Individual and Family Therapy is the result of our desire to share something that has enriched our personal lives as well as therapy and the therapy of those who have taken the time to learn it. This book provides the map that guides therapists to new information about clients, to new guidelines for treatment, and to discoveries about the interaction of the sibling positions of therapists and clients.

Acknowledgments

We wrote this book together, so there is no senior author. Although we each had primary responsibility for certain chapters, we planned the content together, adding ideas and experience as we reviewed and revised each chapter. Bits and pieces of information about sibling positions, garnered from our families, friends, colleagues, students, and clients, are strewn throughout the book. We are indebted to them and the book is richer because of them. We also acknowledge the assistance of our secretaries, Melissa Peterson and Annette Hoxie; without them we would not have completed this book.

Birth Order Roles
&
Sibling Patterns in Individual
&
Family Therapy

The Development of Sibling Position Characteristic Response Patterns

Siblings develop unique characteristic response patterns according to their sibling position in the family. Because these characteristic response patterns set the stage for interpersonal interactions, a knowledge of these patterns is an invaluable tool for the therapist.

CHAPTER 1
Family Environment

In order to understand sibling positions the therapist must acquire information about the family as a whole, including the multigenerational family, the individual as a subsystem, and the relationships among family members in all subsystems. Because a sibling position is a system within a system (a child in the nuclear family), within a larger system (the extended family), the identification of the four basic sibling position response patterns requires a systems approach. This systems perspective of theoretical concepts from several theories can be integrated to describe how family members interact, how individual and family needs are met, and how families accomplish developmental tasks. These concepts set the backdrop for certain assumptions regarding the ways in which sibling position roles develop and complement each other to serve family needs and goals.

Structure in Family Systems

Assumption: Elements of structure in family systems form the context in which sibling positions develop.

The elements of structure in the family system include membership units, interaction patterns, boundaries (inside and outside the family), rules, roles, and alliances. These concepts are convenient fictions that help the therapist analyze family interactions to make sense out of family processes. In reality, many of the characteristics of structure occur simultaneously and in patterns.

Membership Units

The basic family system is the nuclear family, consisting of one or two parents and children. It is a system because of the interconnectedness of family members, who mutually influence each other. This family system contains a number of subsystems, which are organized units within the family that create their own goals, rules, and boundaries in order to maintain themselves. The major subsystems in the family are individuals, dyads, and triads. Each member of the family simultaneously belongs to different subsystems that serve a variety of functions in both the subsystem and the larger extended family system. In addition, the multigenerational family system interacts with societal systems, such as neighbors, friends and peers, schools, churches, work, government, and other social groups.

Interaction Patterns

Individuals and families respond to particular life experiences in their family systems in repetitious ways that become observable, identifiable behavioral patterns. Parents and children develop interaction patterns that are reflected in such things as discipline, recreation, and family chores. These patterns are influenced by family and individual attitudes, role models, thought processes, and the context of learning experiences. Because of their redundancy, the patterns developed by sets of families, sets of individuals, one specific family, one specific subsystem, or one specific individual are called characteristic response patterns. Although families, subsystems, and individuals may be alike in some patterns, they may be very distinct and unique in others.

Boundaries

Certain interaction processes establish boundaries to control the movement of information, people, and objects in and out of systems. Perceptual filters that maintain a given family form boundaries that make it possible for the unit to establish its purposes or goals. Every relationship configuration (i.e., individuals, dyads, triads, families, and societal systems) has these perceptual filters or boundaries. The existence of these boundaries around each relationship configuration in the family allows its members to socialize each other and to adopt values, expectations, and emotional moods that make them different from members of other relationship configurations and families. Without these boundaries, each relationship configuration and each family would lose its identity. For example, the boundary around the marital dyad teaches children that their parents participate in many activities in which children cannot participate. Similarly, two older siblings may form a dyadic relationship with a boundary that isolates a younger sibling.

Boundaries are hierarchical in the sense that some individuals or subsystems have more power and responsibility than others. In nuclear families, this is most easily observed in the parent-child relationship, with the parent in power. Extended families have hierarchical boundaries that influence individual and system development, but also regulate the content of intergenerational transmissions. Normally, as individuals and families move through development stages, hierarchical boundaries change; power and responsibility shift as individuals mature and as their generation moves from one level to another. In order for this shift to occur, however, children must accept responsibility for themselves as they become young adults, rather than shifting this responsibility from their parents to another person, such as a spouse. Hierarchical and other family boundaries influence family rules and roles to create interaction patterns unique to each sibling position.

Rules

All families have rules that govern family and individual behavior. Every family develops rules for the division of labor, power, and money; the provision of emotional support; and the performance of other functions necessary to carry out the tasks of daily life. In their interactions family members develop rules that regulate the expression of emotions, trust, intimacy, dependency, and autonomy in all relationships.

Rules may be explicit or implicit. Explicit rules are those that are known and discussed, such as the time that children are to return home. In contrast, implicit rules have not been verbalized although they may be recognized and followed by everyone. For example, family members may consistently sit in the same places at the dinner table without ever having discussed it. Family members follow some implicit rules without awareness. For example, parents may discipline their children in the same ways that they themselves had been disciplined and be unaware of the repetitions or the reasons for them. Thus, family members may not be able to discuss rules in a logical explicit way, but the repetitiveness of their behavioral patterns indicates the existence of rules beyond cognitive awareness.

From a consistent adherence to rules emerge behavior patterns that help the system to maintain a balance or status quo. When behaviors go beyond the boundaries and rules, the family and its members act to bring the system back into balance either by following the old rules or by developing new ones. The maintenance of balance or survival of the structure is one purpose or goal of the family rules. As siblings enter the family system, they are influenced by the mosaic of family rules.

Roles

The interaction of roles with rules further defines the form of relationships. Certain expected patterns of behavior, permitted as well as forbidden, develop into roles that serve the family system or subsystems. These roles are closely aligned and interactive with system goals, values, and expectations.

Roles may be assumed and assigned explicitly or implicitly. Moreover, the same role may have both explicit and implicit aspects. For example, the father may have had the role of decision maker for all major decisions in the family. The mother may explicitly acknowledge his role, assume that he is also the primary disciplinarian in the family, and assign him that role on an implicit level. The father may be aware of this second role and perform the associated tasks well but never acknowledge the role explicitly. Conflicts arise when people do not fulfill their role in ways that meet the expectations of other family members, either because they are unaware of their family's expectations or because they choose not to meet them. The more implicit the conflict about unmet expectations, the more dysfunctional the conflict may be.

Some role assignments are temporary, continuing only as long as the system needs the role, as long as the person is in the system, or as long as the person is willing to serve the system in that role. Other role assignments are permanent, although the execution of these roles changes as the family and family members change developmentally. These permanent roles are exercised in various contexts (e.g., family of origin, dating, marriage, parenting, socializing, and working) but are not necessarily active all the time. For example, parents of children who live at home may give advice and supply money or support on a continuing basis, but adult children usually require this kind of parenting only in emergencies.

Sibling position roles are complex permanent roles that are assigned at both explicit and implicit levels of awareness. As children enter a particular family organization, they sense the physical, social, and emotional values associated with a specific role for them, and they then develop characteristic response patterns to fulfill their roles. They learn the kinds of behaviors needed to assume the role from the flow of information across various subsystem boundaries, which is governed by relationship rules.

The role of each sibling position is created to meet both the family's and individual's needs. The family system encourages the continuance of the role to meet its needs for productivity and stability. The individual who has assumed the role seeks to maintain the behaviors crucial to the role and does not allow anyone else to assume the same role. It becomes the individual's contribution to the family system and fulfills his or her needs to belong, to be unique, and to make sense and order out of the family environment. Furthermore, the behavior that siblings learn from functioning in the family in their sibling position roles becomes an integral part of their functioning in other contexts, such as school, work, among friends, and later in their own families.

Alliances

Attempts to deal with the issues of authority, power, and emotional support often lead to the formation of alliances among family members. An alliance is an implicit agreement between two or more people to give emotional support to each other or to secure greater power. The first alliance in a family is the marriage, as two people agree to create a nuclear family system within the context of the larger multigenerational family.

As children enter the nuclear system, the potential for additional alliances within the family increases. Parent-child and sibling alliances are natural products of the birth of children into the system, for example. As newborn children have more and more opportunities to interact with their family systems and subsystems, they sense through both explicit and implicit processes the existence of alliances. The messages received about these alliances and about the needs of the total system formulate the role assignment for sibling positions.

Information Processing

Assumption: The family and its subsystems process information that leads to the development of unique sibling positions.

The exchange of information between units within the family and between family and society is the process that maintains the family's structure. The way in which information flows indicates several levels of relationship configurations within the family, such as the marital subsystem, the parent-child and sibling subsystems, the family system, and the individuals themselves. Each of these relationship configurations exists within boundaries, both physical and psychological, that distinguish it from its environment. The family and its subsystems also interact with larger systems, such as extended families, schools, churches, work settings, governments, and communities. The exchange of information across the boundaries of these units must be regulated if each unit is to maintain its identity.

Relationship Channels for Information Flow

Family members process information in six basic channels or directions: (1) *Internal dialogue*. Individuals process information internally about their impressions of others, their beliefs about appropriate behavior in given situations, their self-image, their function in relationships, and their beliefs about the thoughts of other people both inside and outside the family. (2) *Two-person relationships*, such as the husband-wife, parent-child, and child-child subsystems. (3) *One individual and another dyadic relationship.* For example, a child who observes his father and mother arguing responds in some way, if only through his behavior, and his parents are affected by his response. (4) *The family and the individual.* At a family council meeting, for example, individuals give feedback to the family about their perception of the family system and its operation. (5) *Society and the individual.* Each family member exchanges information with school, work, and other societal systems. (6) *The family as a whole group and society.* All families seek to present certain images (e.g., status, wealth, and health) to their neighborhood, their church group, or other outside systems.

The exchange of information along each of these channels is reciprocal and involves complicated processes of language, thought, and behavior, both implicit and explicit. The information present in each relationship configuration teaches individuals how to make their own unique contribution to fulfilling the purposes of the family. In other words, information exchanges along all six relationship structures teach a child to adopt the role of a particular sibling position.

Dimensions of Information Processes

Cognitive and affective messages, perceptual orientation, and verbal and nonverbal behaviors are dimensions of information processes within families. Cognitive and affective language helps derive meaning from the environment. No message is complete without both aspects, as both thoughts and feelings influence the ways in which individuals and families interact.

Every individual has a unique perceptual orientation that is derived from his or her early experiences in life and is used to make sense of how the world works from that individual's viewpoint. All information given and received is screened and analyzed through this perceptual orientation. Because no two people have an identical perceptual orientation in that they have different and unique patterns of emphasis on cognitive and affective processes, those who experience the same event may perceive it differently.

Nonverbal behavior greatly influences the affective and cognitive parts of messages. Voice tone, eye contact or lack of it, touch, body position, and gestures help articulate feelings as part of the message. Some family members may totally attend to nonverbal messages, completely ignoring verbal messages. Others may pay attention only to verbal parts of the message, completely ignoring the nonverbal components. An imbalance in any of these parts of communication creates confusion in family functioning, however, because it distorts information processing.

Emotional experiences consist of physiological responses and cognitive interpretations of the experiences that create labels for the emotions. Individuals may process emotional experiences very differently. Children learn in their families that some ways of dealing with their emotions are acceptable, but others are not. For example, some families view the expression of anger as unacceptable and spend a great deal of time teaching children to suppress anger; in these families it is difficult for family members to discover each other's feelings. In other families, it may be permissible for emotions to surface and for children to learn to express them in acceptable ways. Thus, the slamming of a door may be assumed to be an expression of anger; refusing to talk to someone, an expression of hurt; and fixing a special meal, an expression of love. Without some cognitive message accompanying these expressions of emotion, they can be interpreted differently than was intended.

The appropriate expression of emotion not only permits family members to meet each others' needs, but also allows intimacy to develop in relationships. The way that family members act on their basic emotions is a crucial variable in the healthy functioning of a family. The exchange of information about individuals and relationships in the family, including subsystems, becomes a way of maintaining stability in the family so that family and individual goals can be met. Therefore, some role assignments in the family include maintenance of emotional stability facilitating an explicit expression of emotions, both verbally and nonverbally. Other role assignments focus more on the cognitive aspects of messages and include responsibility for determining details and issues embedded in the message. Thus, perceptual orientation is likely to be somewhat different for the various sibling positions.

Implicit and Explicit Information

Together explicit and implicit information form the Gestalt of information in human interaction. Explicit information (e.g., facts) is straightforward, whereas implicit information (e.g., values) remains embedded in the Gestalt and is more subtle. Implicit information can be made explicit, however, by giving it more distinct emphasis than it had when it was embedded in the interaction of the family. For example, someone in the family may express verbally and directly emotion that had been felt, but never expressed in the past.

Individuals in the family have at different times different levels of awareness about the environment around them. Sometimes, family members have a very distinct, explicit awareness that allows them to explain the motivation behind their behavior or to connect their feelings to some logical happening in the family. At other times, however, these same family members may have only an implicit awareness of the many factors that influence their behavior. They may, for example, experience emotion but lack cognitive awareness of the purpose of the emotion or of the family events that led up to the feeling.

Both explicit information and implicit information are necessary for the healthy functioning of families. Individuals and subsystems in the family may focus more on one kind of information than on the other, however. For example, one child may focus on explicit verbal expressions to make sense out of interactions, whereas another child may focus on the underlying implicit emotional messages.

The Multigenerational Family

Assumption: The sibling position combinations in all generations of the multigenerational family influence the development of the sibling position of each individual.

Members of the nuclear family system are influenced by the larger family system of three or more generations within which they are born and live. Therefore, multigenerational processes affect the interactions of the various sibling position characteristic response patterns. For example, the inheritance of a first child whose parents are both first children and whose grandparents are second and fourth children differs from a first child whose father is a fourth child, whose mother is a first child and whose grandparents are third and fifth children. These effects are transmitted from one generation to another.

Stages of Development

Assumption: Individuals, subsystems, the nuclear family, and the larger intergenerational family simultaneously move through stages of change or development. The issues with which each of these various units are coping at a given time provide part of the unique context into which each sibling is born.

Just as individuals move through many stages of development from infancy through childhood and adolescence to adulthood, nuclear and multigenerational family systems and subsystems move through stages of development. With each major transition new issues surface and require adaptations. Thus, the developmental stages of the individual, couple, and nuclear family interact within the range of the multigenerational system and the societal system to help define the stages of development for the larger and more complex system. This multilevel balancing of development stages is an integral part of the family environment into which each sibling is born. It is a mosaic that influences the role assignment for each sibling position.

Family and Individual Needs

Assumption: Family needs (e.g., to be productive and stable) and individual needs (e.g., to belong, to make sense and order of the world, and to form an identity unique and separate from that of others) are particularly important to the development of sibling positions.

Participation in a family induces members to interact in a manner that allows something of shared value to be derived from the system. This condition creates two reciprocally related levels of purpose in a family system: (1) the family as a whole must meet individual needs of its members, and (2) each family member must interact with the group as a whole and in subsystems to meet the family needs for productivity and stability.

Most families are oriented toward needs associated with survival, such as food, shelter, and physical security. When a man and a woman create a new family through their marriage, the expectations and values of husband and wife result in a need to produce outcomes that represent their union. Such outcomes include acquiring a home, earning material goods, being successful, and having children to fulfill both parents' expectations (as well as the expectations of preceding generations). Children can help meet this need for productivity, as they eventually provide extra help and energy to meet family tasks and goals.

Stability involves the ways or processes by which family goals are met. It includes not only the ways in which things get done, but also the emotional support provided to family members and the general atmosphere of the home. Stability is interwoven within the interactions of all family members, including all those in subsystems, contributing to successful outcomes in relationships. For example, if a family's implied purposes are to express emotion, to achieve an equal distribution of power, and to affirm specific values, then the achievement of these states determines productivity; the way in which these states are achieved (e.g., with negotiation) reflects the stability of the family in any given context. Family concerns with productivity and stability, both implicit and explicit, indicate the conditions that should exist for the well-being of the family and provide the context for meeting the family members' individual goals.

Role assignments for new family members are determined by the balance of productivity and stability in the system at the time of their entry into the family. The family must continually be concerned about reaching its goals, but doing so in a stable way. For example, the family's need for productivity may be enormous, but it cannot be met at the expense of a child's needs because this would create an imbalance between the needs of the child and the needs of the family system. Likewise, a child's needs cannot be met at the disruption and expense of needs of the family as a whole.

As families grow in size, both their organizational complexity and the need for stability increase. Furthermore, needs of the family system are emphasized at different stages of the family life cycle. Thus, as children are born into the family system at different times, each has a different experience because of variations in the family's stability and productivity needs, number of people in the system whose needs must be balanced, developmental tasks, and interactions with societal groups.

Concurrent with the family's needs for productivity and stability are the needs of individuals, both parents and children. Children need to find a place to belong (dependency, intimacy), to relate uniquely (individuality), to discover what they can contribute, and to make sense and order of their environment. Parents have much the same needs in the context of marriage, parenting, and work. While one of the purposes of a family system is to meet these personal needs, families vary a great deal in their efforts to do so. In healthy families, patterns of attachment behavior reflect nurturance, affection, caring, and loyalty. In dysfunctional families, however, these same patterns become scenes of hate, guilt, and retribution. Both attachment patterns are intense, and their influence pervades whole lifetimes.

Clearly, the effectiveness of a family system is determined by members' performance of their ascribed roles relating to family needs for productivity and stability, the extent to which individual goals and needs are met by satisfactory interactions in the system, and the ability of the system to adapt to new information and developmental changes.

Interface between Individual and Family Needs

Assumption: The interface between individual and family needs forms the context in which issues of belonging, loyalty, intimacy, identity, and dependency evolve.

The needs of individuals, subsystems, and the entire family system constantly interact with one another. Most healthy family systems and individuals have legitimate needs that complement each other and can be satisfactorily fulfilled. Sometimes, however, needs of the various membership units cannot be met within the same time frame and conflict arises. For example, parents may need their child to excel in school, which conflicts with the child's need to excel in sports. Issues such as belonging, intimacy, identity, dependency, self-esteem, and autonomy surface as a natural result of the interaction between the needs of individuals, subsystems, and the family. Each unit in the family must resolve the question, "How can my [our] needs be met within the context of the needs of the family and its various subsystems?"

The constant interplay of individual and family needs is a natural byproduct of the complexity of family life. Individuals and families cannot escape the struggle required to balance the demands for simultaneous fulfillment of needs of individuals, subsystems, and families, and this struggle influences the assignment of role characteristics for each sibling as he or she enters the family.

Belonging and Loyalty

Children need to belong, to be cared for, and to understand their role in the family system. The need to belong to the family system continues throughout life but takes on different forms of fulfillment as the family and its individual members move through various stages of development. Individual family members must find ways to belong that meet the family's needs, and the family and its subsystems must find ways to meet the individuals' needs to belong by including them in various relationships and activities.

As family members begin to meet some of their needs outside the family, issues of individual or subsystem autonomy versus loyalty to the family system begin to surface. For example, a mother may take a job that requires her to assume responsibilities and to form relationships outside the family, making her less available to family members. Children may ask to take friends on family outings or vacations; older children may lose interest in long-accepted family activities, preferring to do something with their peers. Because issues around belonging and loyalty often develop at implicit levels of awareness, family members may not discuss the real issues, but rather argue about money, about possessions and whose turn it is to use them, about whether they like their friends better than other family members, about never having time for individuals in the family or the family as a whole, or about changing and becoming a different person. The activities that move family members in and out of the family are normal outcomes of family and individual development, but they add to the complexity of meeting both individual and family needs.

Intimacy

The belonging and intimacy needs of young children are met quite easily if parents and other family members are nurturing and caring. As children grow older, however, intimacy issues become more complicated. Older children may feel uncomfortable snuggling with their parents and other family members. Their intimacy concerns may be more focused on their changing body and decisions about touching and being touched by those outside the family. Issues of self-disclosure also emerge as parents and children struggle to determine the amount of information to share with each other as the family moves through stages of development.

Identity

Individuals' conceptions of the value of their roles in the family and in societal contexts form their identity. Their self-esteem, the composite of their own evaluations in their various roles, is positively affected when they feel that their performance is adequate and that others in the family care about their needs. Their self-esteem is negatively affected when they are critical of their own role performances and others fail to confirm their contributions to the family.

Every family member asks identity questions (e.g., "How am I unique?") and self-esteem questions (e.g., "Do I make a contribution to the family? Who values me for what? Am I lovable and worthwhile?"). These questions also involve issues of intimacy and dependency. Thus, personal identity within the family evolves in part from the interaction of identity, intimacy, and dependency issues. In their journey to adulthood, children struggle to separate from the family and form a clear identity and purpose in life.

Dependency

Sometimes people must rely on others to meet their needs because they either cannot or choose not to do it themselves. Infants, for example, are totally dependent on their parents, older siblings, and extended family to care for their needs. Gradually, as they master developmental tasks, they experience four stages of dependency: (1) total dependency, (2) counter-dependency, (3) independency, and finally (4) interdependency. As needs for dependency change over the life cycle of individuals, various subsystems and the family as a whole must develop their own limits on the degree of dependency that will be allowed. The family must find ways to adapt to the changing needs of individuals for dependency in order to remain functional.

Intergenerational Transmission

Assumption: The multigenerational system's patterns and influences are stored, transformed, and manifested in the three-plus generational family system. Thus, individuals are influenced by the past events and emotional undercurrents of earlier family generations.

All parts of the family, including the extended family, are affected by the other parts. Furthermore, all the generations that have preceded multigenerational family systems have transmitted behavior patterns and information through the family system. Each individual, subsystem, nuclear family, and multigenerational family builds new patterns but also follows some of the old patterns. Sibling response patterns are part of the old and new transmissions, as they affect and are affected by the current system and subsystems. The juxtaposition of the old and the new patterns generates a Gestalt of transmissions to be passed on to future generations at both the implicit and explicit levels of awareness.

Children are forever indebted to their parents for the gift of life and for the care that they receive from infancy to adulthood. Thus, the loyalty issues that surface as children, particularly adolescents, attempt to differentiate from the family may be heavily influenced by intergenerational transmissions. For example, a teen-ager may be receiving conflicting messages from two extended families about the appropriate way to separate from the nuclear family.

Other debts and obligations may accumulate in the multigenerational system and become quite a burden to both parents and children. Sacrifices that mean a great deal to one generation may lose their importance in their transmission to younger generations, but the older generation's expectation for some kind of retribution may be part of the ledger of debts. For example, a father who was unable to go college because he had to work to support his family of origin may be very eager for his children to go to college. He may imply that if they do not attend college they are failing him in some vital way, which makes them feel obligated and burdened. These kinds of messages in the family environment influence family patterns.

Assumption: Siblings are influenced by the unresolved emotional issues of their parents, and may implicitly or explicitly assume responsibility for them.

Family myths, rituals, loyalties, obligations, expectations, and secrets develop naturally over time and are transmitted throughout the multigenerational system. Family members frequently adhere to explicit traditions connected to myths and obligations, without being aware of the implicit meanings. In actuality, these traditions often carry unresolved emotional issues brought to the nuclear family by one or both parents. Incongruous boundaries, secrets, parentification, and myths are only part of the new family's inheritance from the older generations. The inability to communicate and act productively around these vital issues often results from lack of awareness of the unresolved emotional issues in the parents and extended family members. In the roles assigned when they enter the family, children often sense the unresolved emotional issues of their parents, feel responsible for them, and try in some way to achieve resolution.

Multigenerational transmissions are part of the system that greets each new sibling in the family, thus becoming part of the context that shapes the role assignments given to that sibling. The way in which a sibling deals with intergenerational transmissions is influenced by how the sibling perceives the message, how it fits with the responsibilities that the sibling performs for the family system, and how the message from the multigenerational system meshes with personal needs.

CHAPTER 2

Sibling Positions in a Changing Family Environment

A multitude of variables affect the family environment, promoting a constant flux in family interaction and influencing the nature of sibling positions as additional children join the existing family structure.

Uniqueness of the Family Environment

Assumption: The uniqueness of the family environment at the time of each child's birth shapes the characteristic response patterns for each sibling position.
The number of individuals already in the family and the exchanges of affection, behavior, and information among them create a distinctive and unique family environment for each child who enters the family. The changes in the family environment associated with the arrival of a new family member require different responses from family members to meet existing needs. As a result, each child assumes a unique role in the family, called a sibling position.

Although no sibling position is exclusively concerned with any one role, need, or issue in the family system, each sibling has a priority assignment for controlling, maintaining, and influencing certain aspects of the family. As part of family patterns, each sibling develops unique, repetitive, observable, descriptive sibling position characteristic response patterns. The patterns also reflect nonobservable emotions and motivations.

Influential Factors in the Family Environment

Several factors influence the family environment: the balance between family and individual needs, the complexity of the system, the stages of family and individual development, the focus of the family environment, and dysfunctional and functional family patterns.

Balance between Family and Individual Needs

Assumption: In balancing family and individual needs, all family members develop characteristic patterns of responses, some of which influence the development of sibling position characteristic response patterns.

The addition of children to the family increases the family's needs for productivity and stability, but complicates the family's ability to meet these needs adequately. Relationships and services that were once simple become more complex. Family patterns require more cooperation and the execution of a greater variety of roles by family members in accomplishing even basic tasks, such as preparing meals and setting the table. Thus, as productivity needs multiply, additional stability services are required to establish effective communication and to ensure family and personal satisfaction with the quality of life.

As children enter the family system, new roles develop or old ones take on new dimensions to serve the family system as a whole and its various subsystems. The constancy of roles and the ability of family members to adapt to shifting conditions without basic role failures give stability to the family through all the changes that occur. The family concerns for productivity and stability indicate to family members the conditions that must exist for the maintenance of the system. Children receive immediate and continuous information about the system roles in which they must function in order to meet family and individual needs.

Several individual needs are particularly influential in developing sibling position responses. The needs of children to have a sense of belonging to the families in which they are born, to be accepted as important to the system, and to learn to be intimate through relationships within the family continue to manifest themselves through adolescence and adulthood. Children also need to feel that they are unique and separate from the family and that the family recognizes and accepts their contributions to the family system. Messages from the family that accept their separateness from the family as legitimate and affirm their contributions add to their sense of well-being.

The existence of these dual needs (i.e., the need for a sense of belonging and the need for uniqueness and separateness) often causes conflict both in the individual and in other family members. For example, parental concern about a child's spending the night away from home for the first time may be interpreted by the child as a request to stay home and take care of the parents. The child then experiences conflict between a perceived family need (a parental request to stay home that gives approval and credence to the child as a family member) and an individual need (a desire to interact with others outside the family, which may be interpreted as disloyalty to the family).

All family members respond to changing demands by adapting their roles to balance the needs in their family. This balancing begins during courtship and continues into the early marriage. With the birth of the first child, the husband and wife confront new demands for both productivity and stability; they must adjust their role assignments to meet the demands. For example, they must decide who will assume major responsibility for the care of the child. If the wife has been working, she may decide to stay home in order to care for the child. Therefore, a shift occurs in the marital partners' balance of productivity and stability needs. Such shifts affect family messages and, consequently, the roles that siblings assume in families and the characteristic response patterns that develop from those roles.

As the family grows in size, all members of the family participate in the balancing of needs. They do this in various states of awareness, while needs fluctuate in variety and intensity within individuals, relationships, configurations, and the family as a whole. Sometimes attention is focused directly on individual or family needs; at other times, it is focused on the interaction of the two levels of needs. In dealing with the interface dynamic, one family member may defer or give up the fulfillment of a personal need to meet a family need. This focus on the family need does, however, interact with the individual's needs to belong in the family and be accepted by family members. The interface between the two levels of needs, individual and family, is a major influence on the characteristic response patterns for each sibling position in the family system.

Complexity of the System

Assumption: Changes in the complexity of the family system at any given time influence the development of the roles for specific sibling positions.

As the system becomes more complex with the entry of new family members, demands for interaction multiply. The diversity of interactions increases as family members decide with whom to interact, how many to talk to at once, and what to discuss. With the creation of more triangles there is a greater potential for the formation of coalitions and the isolation of individuals. On the other hand, the variety of dyads and triangles provides rich opportunities for individuals to belong and make unique contributions to the family.

The first child born into what was a two-person system becomes an observer, interactor, and reactor to the personalities and the relationship of the parents. The interaction of the first child and the parents transforms the system into a "new family," because family and individual needs, attitudes, values, expectations, information processing, and interaction patterns are all modified with the entry of the child into the family system. The family life experience of each successive child is markedly different because of the transformation and adjustment of existing family members; of the marital, parent-child, and sibling relationships; and of total family interactions.

Before the arrival of the first child, the marital dyad is quite simple. It has three units: two individuals (i.e., husband and wife) and one interactive unit (i.e., the couple dyad). When the first child enters the family, there are seven units (see Table 2–1): three individuals (i.e., mother, father, and one child) and four interactive units (i.e., three dyads and one triangle). Family roles become more numerous for the couple, as the wife is now a mother and the husband is now a father. The role of the spousal subsystem becomes more complex, as it also becomes a parental subsystem. As the parents fulfill their roles, the first child learns that some of his or her personal needs will be met by the parents. As the parents respond to their first child, they learn how to be parents and how to continue to be spouses, even with the added responsibilities of parenthood.

When the first child is born, parents are inexperienced and uncertain about their ability to raise a child. The need to learn the skills of caring for a child, balance responsibilities both in and out of the home, and find quality time for the marital relationship often creates tension and anxiety between the mother and father, and sometimes between the parents and the child. Because of the importance and newness of their experiences, parents place significantly more pressure for achievement on their first child. Furthermore, the child is expected to be an example for siblings that follow and later may assume some of the parenting role for younger siblings.

The entry of the second child into the family again increases the number of units, variety of roles, and thus the number of individual and family system needs. The nuclear family now contains 14 units: four individuals (i.e., mother, father, and two children) and 10 interaction units of six dyads and

Table 2–1 The complexity of the family system.

Interaction units	First child	Second child	Third child	Fourth child
Individuals	3	4	5	6
Dyads	3	6	10	14
Triangles	1	4	10	20
Total	7	14	25	40

four triangles. In addition to the spousal and parental subsystems, there is a sibling subsystem in that each sibling now has not only the role of son or daughter, but also the role of brother or sister. The family responds to the increased complexity of the system by adding roles and expecting more in performance of existing roles.

Because some of the tasks of parenting, such as feeding, bathing, and changing a baby, have become routine skills, parents are less anxious about their ability to succeed as parents with the second child. Parents, therefore, become more consistent with their discipline and are more likely to dispense warm, supportive responses on a continuous, noncontingent basis than they are with the first child.

The number of family units increases from 14 to 25 with the arrival of the third child; the nuclear family has five individuals (i.e., mother, father, and three children) and 20 interaction units (i.e., 10 dyads and 10 triangles). The entry of the fourth child into the family system brings the number of units to 40: six individuals and 24 interaction units (see Table 2–1).

With two children, parents can each take one child, or one parent can quite easily manage two children. With three or four children, however, it is impossible for the parents to focus individually on each child at the same time; in fact, it is difficult for the parents to find time to interact with everyone. Moreover, it is difficult to meet transportation needs and perform care-giving tasks as the older children become more involved with friends and activities outside the family. The sibling system increases in size and in demands for new relationships. Because of the time demands on the parents, older siblings are given additional roles that serve the family and subsystem, such as a parental helper in caring for younger children.

The increased complexity of the family that occurs with the entry of new members changes the interactions of the family by modifying pattern sequences to incorporate the new members, by necessitating new rules or changes in old rules to cover new situations and different needs, and by modifying roles or adding new ones. Changes within marital, parental, and sibling subsystems reflect these modified patterns, rules, and roles. With the transformation and adjustment of the roles of different family members, siblings are affected by the order of their births and the changing conditions in the family environment. Each sibling assumes a unique role to serve the family system and develops characteristic response patterns within that role.

Stages of Family and Individual Development

Assumption: Individual, nuclear family, and multigenerational family stages of development interact to contribute to the uniqueness of the family environment for each sibling position.

The interaction of the development stages of individuals, the nuclear family, and the extended family contribute to the complexity of the changing family environment. This multilevel balancing of various developmental stages affects the family environment into which each sibling is born. When the first and second children are born, the parents are moving from the stage of a married couple into the stage of a family with young children. As young adults, they are individuating from their families of origin and establishing their competency in society, in the work force, and in the home as spouses and parents. The extended family is in the stage of launching young adults from their home into society. The developmental stages of all these units are different when third and fourth children enter the family. The marriage is no longer new, parents are no longer inexperienced, and competency issues for them in the work force and society are different. The extended family has launched more children, and the grandparents are moving toward activities of later life.

Focus of the Family Environment

Assumption: Each time a child is added to the family, individuals, subsystems, and the family as a whole respond to the needs of the new family environment with a shift in focus.

Because families are not only part of an extended family but also part of society, they direct their attention to people, issues, things, and events outside the family system as well as inside the system. The major focus of the parents and other family members shifts inward in response to changing system needs and to subsystem complexity when a new child enters the family. An inward focus centers on the needs of the family and family members and ways to meet those needs through productivity and the quality of relationships.

Parents and children must also direct some attention outward, however, to manage the interaction of the family with society. As the older children become involved in school and other activities, the mother and father are also involved in new roles (e.g., chauffeur, PTA officer, Little League coach, and arbitrator of disputes). This focus of parents and older siblings alters the role messages received by each new child. Younger siblings respond to these messages in ways that become part of their characteristic response patterns.

Dysfunctional and Functional Family Patterns

Assumption: A family's functional status, as individuals and as a unit, affects the characteristic response patterns of each sibling position.

The structural, attitudinal, and behavioral patterns of dysfunctional couples and families lack appropriate responses to the needs and goals of the marriage, the family, and individuals. The patterns do not allow for normal interactions among units or normal behavior in individuals. In addition, one or both of the spouses, or one or more of the children, may exhibit symptomatic behavior that may be labeled emotional illness.

In contrast, the structural, attitudinal, and behavioral patterns of functional couples and families promote the achievement of consensual goals and shift appropriately with stress and growth. These patterns allow for normality in the subsystems within the family, in the family as a whole, and in individual members.

In crisis situations, such as death, illness, major economic shifts, divorces, remarriages, major conflict, and shifts in relationships, families and individuals may develop dysfunctional patterns. The roles of siblings who are born into crisis situations or into chronically dysfunctional families are the same as those assigned to siblings in functional families, but they are exaggerated and distorted in some manner. For example, a first child born when the father is out of work and emotionally unstable may become overly responsible, trying to fill the role of an adult, or may appear terribly irresponsible because the job assignment is unreasonable and impossible.

The functional or dysfunctional status of the family is part of the family environment into which each sibling is born. The ways in which siblings perform their roles depend partly on the messages that they receive from the family about their responsibilities for correcting dysfunction in individuals or in the family. Because each sibling receives unique messages about dysfunction, the quality of the family's functioning as a whole and of individual family members' functioning affects each sibling's perception of the world and development of a sense of well-being.

CHAPTER 3

Characteristic Response Patterns for Sibling Positions

Although the characteristic response patterns for sibling positions are holistic, they can be divided into three categories for descriptive purposes: (1) functional family system roles, (2) perceptual orientation, and (3) identity and a sense of well-being.

Functional Family System Roles

Assumption: Siblings are assigned separate, unique, permanent, functional family system roles when they are born into the family.

Each sibling performs specific system roles assigned by the family according to his or her position in the sibling subsystem and assumed by the individual when he or she enters the family. Roles are perceptual-behavioral patterns learned and manifested by an individual in order to ensure the individual's physical and social survival within the family. They are the external manifestations of internal patterns of perception about the ways in which individuals relate to other family members and functionally fit into the entire family system. The roles are functional in that they serve the goals of the family system. Specific role patterns develop that are characteristic of each sibling position. These roles should not be confused with an individual's specific abilities, personal capacities, or activities that are not related to the family system role.

Family-assigned roles are the earliest learned. The family's ability to impose the role on the child is facilitated by the infant's total dependency on the family for physical and psychological survival. Moreover, the older child depends on the family unit to meet the needs to belong and to be accepted as a unique, contributing person. When conflicts arise later between two incompatible role expectations, individuals stubbornly retain those roles derived from early family experience.

Siblings receive family system role assignments on two levels of awareness, implicit and explicit. As infants, children receive the major impressions of their assignments at implicit and unconscious levels. Messages at the implicit level are more easily made explicit than are messages at the unconscious level, because the latter are often attached to dysfunctional survival needs of the adults in the family, nuclear or extended, and may involve a great deal of unexpressed and perhaps unrecognized pain, terror, or fear. Although parents and other family members are explicit about some of their expectations for each sibling, they also communicate their expectations at the implicit level. In spite of the lack of explicit communication, role assignments are functional in that they define the child's responsibilities in the system. Children respond to the messages received and, while serving the family, learn to meet their individual needs through the family and specific family members. Thus, the assignment and acceptance of the role occur at the interface of system and individual needs.

The outward behaviors of the role may change as the child passes through various stages of development and develops a personality commensurate with his or her capabilities and physical, mental, and emotional experiences. The basic responsibilities do not change, however. As the family moves through developmental stages, the need for the role in the family system continues, but the family's perception of the appropriate performance of the role changes. For example, a child is responsible for family rules in a different manner at 6 years of age, at 18, and later at 38.

In order to clarify and describe siblings' functional family system, the patterns can be organized into three subcategories:

1. *Job assignment.* Family job assignments determine in general what siblings are expected to do for the system. Do they serve individuals more than they serve relationships or the system as a whole? Does the job require more emphasis on meeting productivity needs or stability needs?

2. *Interpersonal responsibilities.* Specific interpersonal responsibilities enable siblings to complete their job assignments. For and to whom are they responsible? How do they take care of people? What do they expect from others in the family?

3. *Social interactions.* Social interactions occur with other family members within the context of the family environment. Social interactions are unique to each sibling position and are learned first within the family and later manifested in relationships outside the family. The subcategories interact with each

other to form patterns that represent social responses, including the interactions of siblings in relationships, their responsibilities in the interaction, and their expectations of themselves and others. The success of the siblings' function in their respective roles is correlated with their perceptual orientation and their sense of well- being, or personal identity.

Perceptual Orientation

Assumption: Every sibling position has a perceptual orientation that begins at birth, is heavily influenced by family interaction, and is characteristic of that position.
The need to make sense and order of the world motivates children to develop a way of perceiving it. In this effort, children use all their senses; the cognitive outcome of this integration of the senses is designated as perception. The psychological definition of orientation is an awareness of one's environment as to time, space, objects, and persons. Therefore, perceptual orientation includes both focus and awareness.

Children's view of the world is partially established by the conditions within the family environment, the assignments given to their sibling position, and their individual personality characteristics. Their orientation is affected by their perception of the value and purpose given them by their family. In summary, perceptual orientation is a filtering process that gives each child a unique psychological awareness and adaptation to situations in the environment. Characteristic perceptual orientation patterns are discernible in each sibling position.

The perceptual orientation patterns developed in each sibling position can be organized into three subcategories:

1. *Focus or awareness.* Each sibling focuses on, or is more aware of, certain aspects of the environment. The focus of each sibling is influenced by the focus of the family and by the job assignment. If a sibling's job is to ensure that everyone follows the family rules, for example, focus on the rules and awareness of who does and who does not follow the rules would have to be part of that sibling's perceptual orientation.

2. *Cognitive patterns.* Siblings develop distinctive cognitive patterns that are recognizable in such traits as a focus on details rather than on connections. For example, siblings who are responsible for the whole family system must be able to see how a piece of information fits into the whole in order to understand it.

3. *Affective patterns.* The importance of affect, whether implicit or explicit, and its relative importance to results, issues, and stability within a given context are different for all sibling positions. Affective patterns interact with

role assignments and cognitive perceptions to shape siblings' attitudes about feelings and ways to deal with feelings.

Identity and Sense of Well-Being

Assumption: Every sibling position has an identity and sense of well-being characteristic of that position.

Children develop a set of beliefs about themselves based on how secure they feel, how they affect others, how well they do things, and how much others value them. The needs to be unique, to be an individual, and yet to be valued for who they are and what they contribute to the family guide the formation of their identity. Their beliefs about that identity interact with confirming and disconfirming experiences, at first in the family and later in society, to form their sense of well-being. In response to the interaction of their beliefs and experiences, children develop characteristic response patterns that reflect their positive or negative perception of themselves. These response patterns can be divided into four subcategories for description:

1. *Self-esteem.* The way in which individuals perceive themselves is a vital part of their self-esteem. Issues of belonging, of feeling secure in the family and in other situations, of knowing what to do and when to do it, and of being separate from the family are central to the development of self-esteem. A sense of well-being influences behavior and affective states. From the beginning, children try to create a sense of personal wholeness, as they meet the challenges of living. This is never easy, however, because developmental issues and contextual complexity often create uncertainty, fear, and a sense of being threatened.

2. *Threat to well-being.* All children feel threatened by abandonment; physical, sexual, and verbal abuse; and a lack of positive affirmations from family members. The way in which siblings experience and interpret negative events that threaten their personal security varies according to their sibling position, however. Many threats originate from a combination of beliefs about themselves and explicit and implicit information about their job performance in the family. For example, children whose assigned functional role is to be productive for the family feel threatened when they perceive that their efforts are not noted and accepted by family members. They feel like failures.

3. *Responses to threats to well-being.* Individuals who feel threatened by a situation that is puzzling, abusive, scary, or seemingly unresolvable respond according to their sibling position and to their experiences in functional or dysfunctional systems. When conflicts with other family members threaten them, first children tend to be highly rational, defensive, and very verbal, and they may focus on details and facts about the events surrounding the conflict.

In the same situation, fourth children tend to be highly emotional and irrational, and they may focus on whether others blame them for the conflict.

4. *Siblings' needs from others.* In order to develop an identity and a secure sense of well-being, everyone needs attention, love, and approval from other people. All children in sibling positions, however, also need them in order to do their job assignments. Consequently, siblings often ask for things in ways that are very different, and respond in ways that are just as different when the request is granted or denied. For example, in order to feel worthwhile, fourth children seek verbalizations from family members that verify that they make a difference in the harmony of the family. In contrast, first children need approval and recognition for doing a job correctly.

Variations That Affect Sibling Positions

Assumption: After the fourth sibling, the position patterns begin to repeat, with the responses taking into consideration the increased complexity of the family.

Bach and Anderson (personal communication) noted that the patterns repeat, with some variation, after the first four sibling positions. For this reason, the first four patterns are designated as basic. Fifth children have responses similar to those of first children, sixth children have responses similar to those of second children, and so on. Clinical observations seem to validate the hypothesis of the repetition of patterns, at least for some individuals, but additional research is required to determine the precise characteristics that distinguish between the first four basic birth positions and subsequent birth positions. There are, after all, differences in the family system for later-born siblings. For example, later siblings are born into a more complex system with two sets of parents: (1) the mother and father and (2) two older siblings who are expected to do some of the parenting. Furthermore, the family system is in a different stage of development, parents and siblings are older, and society patterns and values may have changed for the later-borns. System needs and role assignments may repeat themselves, but there remains much to learn about the distinguishing characteristics between the first four basic sibling patterns and the patterns for siblings who follow.

Assumption: Twins and other multiple birth siblings may receive role assignments characteristic of the order in which they are born, or they may receive blurred role assignments.

Because the complexity of the family system is affected by multiple births, whether each child of a multiple birth accepts or is given a basic position or some combination of role assignments can be determined only by clinical observation and research. Each child definitely receives a role assignment from the family, but the determination of which sibling role requires careful examination of the interaction exchanges between each child of the multiple birth and the family system. These children may receive blurred role assignments, some kind of a blend of the sibling positions in question. Observations of a limited number of twins suggest that each twin develops the characteristic response patterns of the sibling position into which he or she is born. For example, the twin who is born first and is the third child in the family assumes the role of the third sibling. Though born but a few minutes later, the twin who is born second assumes the role of the fourth sibling.

Assumption: Spacing of siblings has an unspecifiable effect on the characteristic response patterns for the basic sibling positions.
Research has yet to determine the effects of the number of years between siblings. As therapists, we ask questions to determine if the sibling patterns fit, regardless of the spacing between siblings. It appears that the greater the spacing and the fewer the siblings, the less characteristic some of the patterns. Thus far, however, patterns of differences cannot be specified.

Assumption: The sex of the sibling affects the way in which a role is performed rather than what the role is.
Because the family system characteristics are the same, sibling role assignments are similar regardless of sex. Gender has its greatest effect on the performance of role. Part of the role assignment for the first child is to be responsible for everyone in the family. For example, if the father fails to meet the emotional and sexual needs of his spouse, the first child may be enlisted in dysfunctional ways to meet the mother's needs. The gender of the child determines how the child tries to do this. Clinicians can use all that they know about gender differences in working with each sibling position.

Assumption: Deletions or additions of siblings may alter or blur the role assignments of sibling positions. Likewise, deletions or additions of parents affect the way in which siblings assume their roles.
Deaths of siblings, miscarriages, abortions, adoptions, accidents, prolonged illness, retardation, and other events that delete or add family members lead to variations in normal family development, changing the family environment and the role assignments. Similarly, the presence of step-children, half-brothers, half-sisters, and step-parents changes the family environment and affects the expectations of parents. Unknown events, such as unreported abortions and previous marriages, also influence role assignments for children who enter the family after the events.

When these interruptions in family development occur, siblings may assume some of the roles previously assigned to a sibling who has died or left the family for some reason. Depending on the length of time that the departed sibling was in the family, the way in which the family deals with the absence, and other factors (e.g., secrecy), messages to remaining and later siblings may be confusing. For example, if a miscarriage preceded the birth of their first child, parents prepare for and act differently in the second pregnancy, although the child is not a second child. Thus, the messages received by the child may differ slightly from the messages that would have been received if the miscarriage had not happened, and the child's responsibilities and roles may be blurred. The miscarriage may not be mentioned to later children, which can also cause blurring of roles.

Parental disruptions may also alter the way in which siblings assume their roles and serve the family. Disruptions in the family system caused by a parent's severe illness, physical or emotional incapacity, or absence from the home for an extended time change the signals about system needs and role assignments sent to a sibling at birth. Single-parent families, step-families, foster care, and children cared for by siblings, grandparents, or other adults, all represent settings that may lead to deviations in sibling position characteristic responses. These areas of exception call for research and study.

Assumption: Sometimes characteristic response patterns for two or more sibling positions appear to be similar, but the motivational factors are different.

Because all children have the same needs and exhibit similar responses to similar situations, some response patterns in one of the basic sibling positions may appear to be similar to those in another sibling position. For example, first and second children are alike in their perceptual focus on details and parts. First children are like third children in that each pays less attention to the implicit than to the explicit. Upon examination, however, unique variations that are distinguishable by emphasis and motivation are apparent in the perceived similarities.

First children focus on detail in order to obtain adequate information, thereby reducing the margin for error in their performance of their jobs. They rarely know when they have enough information, so they continue to seek more. In contrast, second children focus on detail in order to determine the underlying structure of the family and to align implicit information with explicit rules. Because of their faith in their ability to understand the underlying structure and implicit information, they are apt to assume that they have enough information when, in fact, they do not. As therapists become more familiar with sibling position patterns, these distinctions will become more apparent.

Four Basic Sibling Positions

The characteristic response patterns of the four sibling positions are functional patterns. They become dysfunctional when they are exaggerated, shut down, or blocked by environmental circumstances. As they begin to study the patterns of each sibling, clinicians tend to forget that all sibling positions have patterns that are very similar. The patterns designated as characteristic patterns tend to stand out as patterns for each sibling position. The fact that first siblings tend to focus first on parts and details, and fourth siblings tend to focus first on the Gestalt of a situation, for example, does not mean that fourth siblings never pay attention to details or that first siblings never get the complete picture.

CHAPTER 4
First-Born Siblings

The hopes, desires, and dreams of parents, as well as those of multiple generations of the family, are carried by the first child. Everything the child does is being done for the first time in the eyes of the parents and the extended family. The first smile, the first tooth, the first steps, the first word, the first day of school, and the first graduation, are all met with elated responses from parents, grandparents, and other relatives. In most cases, the responses from this large family audience are more exaggerated than they will be for any subsequent child.

Functional Family System Roles

First children are assigned functional roles as they enter the family system. These roles include: (1) the job assignment, (2) interpersonal responsibilities, and (3) social interactions.

Job Assignments

Parents sense that their extended family and the outside world watch what their first child does to determine what they are like as a family. Therefore, the dominant message that first children receive is that they are on display and that the family focus is outward. All of this leads first children to feel that they are the central focus and that their actions have consequences far beyond themselves. First children sense that their behavior and words are observed and weighed by others and they, therefore, adopt external validation to evaluate themselves. These same expectations for high-quality performance may also be observable in grandparents and other members of the extended family. Although parents may have high expectations for all their children, the performance of no other child receives quite the same emphasis that the performance of the first child receives.

From this family interaction, first children learn that their job assignment is to produce outcomes that meet with the family's approval. Parents are focused on productivity because of their need to provide for the child the costs of birth, new clothes, furniture, baby supplies, car seat, space, and the future. Therefore, first children focus on the family's need for productivity and do their best to meet that demand.

The product differs somewhat from family to family. From an outsider's viewpoint, first children may not always appear to be productive, but the outsider may not understand what the children perceive as their family's particular need. For example, a first child may work to produce an intangible outcome, such as ensuring that younger siblings obey family rules, planning a family project, or going to a function with their parents. By being productive in these ways, first children represent the explicit parental standards of responsibility, success, and social decorum.

First children are both overachievers and underachievers. Because they find it difficult to determine when they have done enough, they do more than is necessary to accomplish a task. They are underachievers if family expectations are too great and the demands too harsh. They feel impelled to be involved in a task if others think they should be. Usually, they do not admit that they cannot do a task, even if they feel overwhelmed by it, because to do so would thwart the expectations of perceived authority figures, such as parents. They indirectly bring attention to their difficulty, however, by not following through on the project.

Another job assignment for first children is to support and enforce the family's explicit rules and values within the family. In addition, they are expected to support and display family values beyond the family circle to serve the best interests of the family. By enforcing the family's rules and social expectations, they help to uphold the family image, the product seen by the outside world; thus, they serve another productivity function.

First children focus less on the family's stability needs than do younger siblings, because these needs are not as great when first children enter the family as they are when later siblings are born. There are fewer relationship units, and the structure and need for information processing is not as complicated. If stability needs are explicitly discussed as part of a family goal, however, first children respond by trying to produce the desired outcome, the meeting of some stability need. First children are likely to respond to that which is discussed and made explicit.

Interpersonal Responsibilities

Interpersonally, first children work to keep individuals within the family functioning within the rules and parental values. They feel responsible for the individuals in the family rather than for the subsystems or the family as a whole. The following excerpt from a therapy session in which an adult male first sibling described a family incident illustrates the first sibling's focus on individuals.

> So I witnessed a lot of what was going on, rather than participating. That is something that I tend to do rather easily. I have a feeling that I may be more sensitive to individuals one at a time than I am to a group. Even within my own family, I would be more cognizant of something that is bothering this child or that child than I would be of the relationships of one child to another or of the interrelations among three or four, and five and six.

First children are responsible to and for their parents. They are responsible to their parents for such things as siblings, rules, jobs, loyalty, and efforts to meet family expectations. They are responsible for their parents in such things as the parents' unresolved issues, welfare, and happiness.

In family systems, it is impossible to be equally responsible to and for both parents; therefore, the child must choose to be more responsible to and for one parent than the other. The factors that influence this choice are unclear. It appears first children attend to the parent who is most obviously or explicitly carrying out productivity functions in the family. For example, they become responsible to and for the father in traditional homes because his departure for work every morning makes his productivity function explicit and obvious. In homes where productivity functions are reversed or more balanced, or where one parent's productivity is not more explicit than the other's, first children are just as likely to be more responsible to and for the mother.

In systems outside the family (e.g., school, play, and work), first children demonstrate their ability to interpret and follow rules by using "good" and "tried" ideas to get things done. They also appear to be willing to do their share. Sometimes, however, they seem to be rule-bound, rigid, and inflexible in trying to get others to comply with their interpretation of the rules. They have been assigned this role in the family at an implicit level, and they consistently try to do their job, no matter how they are perceived.

First children feel a particular responsibility to live up to the expectations of other significant people, especially authority figures. Those in authority represent the source of approval and are often the voice for explicit rules. Consequently, authority is always an interpersonal issue for first children.

Social Interactions

First children are sociable and interact well with others. Because they interact primarily with adults (until another child is born), they learn many social skills. In particular, they learn from observations of adult interactions the importance of talking well. First children are not always at ease in social interactions, however, because they feel that they must meet the expectations of other people. Performance anxiety accompanies this lack of ease, although first children are masters at covering up their anxiety, perceiving it as a failure. Furthermore, if first children think that others have not had a good time, they blame themselves even when they have no fault in the matter at all. As in other contexts, first children fear that they are inadequate in social settings.

In peer relationships, first children maintain a distinctly separate identity from others. They rarely see themselves as totally involved in a relationship. Rather, they see themselves as very independent and can appear at times not to need anything from the relationship. Since relationships are based on common interests or needs, however, they want to make an important contribution that serves the goals of the relationship. In work and school contexts, first children join with others to achieve some task. With friends, the goal of relationships may be to have fun by playing games, participating in sports, and going to movies or parties. The purpose of personal conversations may be to reach a decision, to stimulate further thinking and ideas, or to produce new information or details. As long as those in the relationship seem to be working to reach its goals, first children are happy and fun to be around. If those in the relationship are not working toward what first children perceive as the goal, however, they may fight, nag, interrupt, criticize, and make unceasing demands to obtain cooperation.

In social situations, first children encourage others to share ideas, information, and feelings (if it is obvious that feelings are important to clarify situations). Sometimes, first children ask too many questions, want too many detailed facts and figures, and continue to search for data that others see as irrelevant. If, however, they become overwhelmed by the amount of detail, they close their minds and refuse to consider additional information. They may include excessive detail in their own conversation, believing additional information adds clarity, but others may be distracted by the detail.

In groups, first children are comfortable as either leaders or members. They like to function as leaders, provided that their function is clear and accepted by others. They are good at soliciting information from the group they are leading, but they may appear pushy at times because of their emphasis on getting the task at hand accomplished. As members, they remain centrally involved as long as they feel they can be influential and that others recognize their contributions. If they feel that the leader is incompetent, or unfair, first children leave the group or enter into a power struggle with the leader. In handling this dilemma about authority, first children may rebel explicitly by disagreeing, objecting to the rules, or confronting the competence of the leader. They may rebel implicitly by appearing to listen and agree, but never doing anything. Although first children are willing to oppose people in authority, they are not often open about it.

When first children feel unrecognized and unimportant or cannot perceive their contribution to the group, they lose interest and either become apathetic or join other groups. First children have been on center stage in the family, so they assume they should serve this same function in groups. They translate their responsibility for productiveness in the family into a responsibility for the productiveness of everyone. Therefore, if a group is not productive, first children feel responsible, even when this feeling appears irrational to others.

If first children feel that they live up to the expectations of others in social interactions, they are happy and engaged. If they feel that they do not meet others' expectations, they can be aloof or so intense in their efforts to secure the approval of others that they become a nuisance. If the power structure in a group or relationship denies opportunities for recognition, first children become highly threatened and may manifest rebellion, defiance, antagonism, underachievement, and withdrawal.

If the marital dyad is weak in the family, first children tend to form coalitions with one parent against the other. If a first child perceives that the father is not fulfilling his responsibilities as a "good" husband, for example, the child may form a coalition with the mother, not necessarily to oppose the father, but to meet some of the mother's needs that the father has failed to meet. First children feel responsible in such a situation and try to compensate the parent's failure.

Perceptual Orientation

In trying to make sense of the world they live in, all children attempt to get a complete picture. Some look at the parts to find the whole, while others examine the whole to identify the parts. First children's perceptual orientations are heavily influenced by the fact that they are born into a small family system.

Three subcategories elaborate the characteristics of first children's perceptual orientation: (1) focus and awareness, (2) cognitive patterns, and (3) affective patterns.

Focus and Awareness

Because the family of the first child is small, he or she can focus explicitly on individuals, parts, and details. Because of the family size, members can spend time with each other and projects. First children adopt this family focus and translate it into a perceptual focus on explicit, observable behavior. By focusing on parts and details, they make sense of the entirety of their world.

First children focus on the rational, rule-governed aspects of reality, using rational, analytical thought to create meaning for what they see in the world. The reason that the first child responds so much to the world in this way is not clear, except that the family interaction observed by the first child consists largely of adult interaction. Adults are verbal and analytical; therefore, the first child learns that it is important to focus on words and facts. In addition, it is probably true that the first thing any young child focuses on is the most explicit and the most observable.

First children find that focusing on detail and explicit information helps them complete a task and fulfill the productivity function that the family assigned. It is not so much that first children do not use other means to make sense of their environment. Rather, they use rationality based on explicit information as their primary means, and other methods are secondary.

Cognitive Patterns

Verbal description is an important part of first children's cognitive patterns. They focus on the semantics of an explanation to determine which words best fit the situation. In fact, their focus on the literal meaning of words is so intense that they may confront and even harass others about the literal meaning of the words they use. The ability to use words with clarity and force is the hallmark of first children's cognitive world.

In terms of noticing, remembering, and using details to make rational decisions, first children are experts. To first children, the whole of something is the sum of its parts, and they come to understand the meaning of various parts by analyzing all the details and facts of the situation. For example, if first children have a task to accomplish, they determine the final product that others expect, break the task down into parts, and finish one part at a time until the entire task is finished. Although they very clearly understand separate ideas and pieces, first children sometimes fail to notice the interrelatedness of the parts unless someone makes it explicit for them.

In their cognitive process, first children think about ideas, tasks, and groups of people by compartmentalizing them. They gather similar kinds of information and sort them into separate, isolated pieces. If they sense that they are missing a piece, they search relentlessly to find it. First children want to know all the facts. They fear that, if anything is omitted, they may not be "on target" with the goal, or they may not be right. If they believe that someone is withholding information, they pester that person until they acquire the information.

Once first children believe that they understand all the pieces and details of a situation, they go to great lengths to defend their explanation of it, presenting information backed by logic and facts. It is sometimes difficult to get them to consider additional information, because they restrict their perceptual field to maintain their own elaborately constructed explanation. First children need to feel that their explanations are right, and being right sometimes becomes more important than considering new information that may make them appear "off target."

When confronted with an ambiguous situation, first children respond analytically, defining the details of the situation and analyzing the expectations. They then establish a structure for achieving a task or making sense of the situation. This gives first children a distinctive place and assures them of results.

Affective Patterns

First children approach feelings through rational cognition. They have to think about their feelings in order to realize their existence and label them. They see feelings important only if they are clearly relevant to reaching outcome; feeling for feeling's sake is not important to them.

First children deny feelings if they believe that the discovery of their emotions by others would make them seem weak, vulnerable, and unproductive. Although they experience a full and varied range of emotions, they may see these feelings as irrelevant to their productivity function, or they may simply fail to focus on them because they are implicit rather than explicit. At other times, they may see the expression of emotions as a violation of the social rules under which they should operate.

First children experience a great deal of anxiety about their own performance and the approval of others. They usually have some anger; because they believe that their efforts to be productive have never been quite sufficient. They also feel guilty when they find themselves involved in so many things that they are overwhelmed and cannot be responsible for everything and everybody. Even then, however, first children assume that they should be able to do all things.

First children become confused unless they can break everything into parts to be dealt with one at a time. This confusion is accompanied by a fear that they will be unable to perform because they cannot make sense of all the pieces. Too often, their strategy for dealing with too much detail is to seek more information in the belief that additional detail will make everything clear. In such situations, first children need feedback that enough is enough.

In the family, first children may pick up messages intended for the parent for whom they feel most responsible and act as if the messages are their own. If they feel responsible for the father, they often exhibit his unexpressed pain and anger; they rarely connect it to the father, however, unless he clearly and explicitly explains his emotions. Similarly, first children may act out their father's unexpressed fantasies and wishes. For example, if the father is angry with a member of the family and does not resolve this himself first children may take on the father's battle without being aware that they are fighting to resolve their father's issues.

Identity and Sense of Well-Being

The characteristic response patterns for identity and sense of well-being for first-born siblings can be divided into four subcategories: (1) self-esteem, (2) threats to well-being, (3) responses to threats to well-being, and (4) sibling's needs from others.

Self-Esteem and Well-Being

For first children, self-esteem is based on doing well in the eyes of others and behaving in socially appropriate ways. They feel valued and appreciated on the basis of their productivity and others' recognition of their competence. This feeling of self-worth lasts for only short periods at a time, however. After the accomplishment of each task, first children must achieve other outcomes in order to continue to feel worthwhile. Their self-esteem is often based more on what they can do than on who they are.

In order to have high self-esteem, first children need to feel central and involved in achieving their own goals and in meeting the expectations of those people who are significant to them in the context in which they are functioning. First children also need to feel that they are right in the methods they choose to reach the outcomes that are important to them and to these significant other people. They have a powerful set of internal values that they use in assessing the worth of what they do. The most important identity question for first children is "Do the people who are important to me approve of what I can do?"

Threats to Well-Being

The most obvious threats to the well-being of first children are implicit and explicit messages that their performance is inadequate. Verbal messages of disapproval are definitely threatening to first children; moreover, they often assume that the absence of feedback indicates disapproval. First children feel threatened and lose their sense of well-being when they cannot obtain enough information to satisfy themselves or when there are so many details that they cannot understand everything.

Some first children assume that they must do everything themselves. When the task if overwhelming, they worry and fret, but they seldom admit that they cannot complete the task alone. They keep their anxiety and frustration totally to themselves.

When parents leave first children alone often and for long periods of time, their well-being is threatened. Without external validation, they are forced to focus on what they perceive as an inadequate self. Hours of crying, intense hurt, and feelings of abandonment develop defenses of analytical, nonfeeling behaviors.

Responses to Threats to Well-Being

First children who experience chronic disapproval from the people in their environment feel like failures and experience life as hopeless. Amid impossible expectations and frequent disapproval of what they do, first children become discouraged and cease producing. In response to a single instance of disapproval, however, they may first argue that the evaluation is inaccurate. Once they accept the evaluation, they try harder the next time to prove their importance and worth, although they continue to worry about whether what they are doing will meet with approval.

When first children are highly threatened, they feel angry at everybody and everything, but they handle the anger by retreating inside. They appear dark, unapproachable, immovable, and even unfeeling. In reality, however, they are angry, frightened, and sad—although they deny these feelings. Accompanying such emotions are a sense of responsibility for something that did not work, indignation at the "unjust" evaluation, and terror that everyone will abandon them in disapproval. If someone pushes them when they feel threatened, first children are likely to explode with great emotional intensity. If the threat is resolved in a constructive way, they may later be able to admit their feelings.

First children become extremely dogmatic when threatened. Insisting that they are right, they use verbal arguments to convince others of their position. They are experts at using their verbal skills to extricate themselves from difficult situations. They often use verbosity to manipulate others and to keep others away from core central issues. For example, if first children know that they must explain why a task has not been finished, they construct detailed verbal explanations. In other situations, they may spend a great deal of time talking about something that is irrelevant to the real issue. In their minds, verbosity hides their imperfections from others.

First children who feel threatened withdraw from other people if they believe that it would be fruitless to initiate a direct confrontation or that there is no way for them to be right in an argument. When someone else initiates a confrontation under these circumstances, first children respond either with a complex, rational argument or with vagueness. Often they argue about the semantics, the meaning of words, or the details. Vagueness is usually an attempt to keep the other person from discovering the details and perceiving their performance as inadequate.

Siblings' Needs from Others

First children need to receive explicit recognition from others for what they do. They need to feel approval for being productive. Any type of feedback that focuses on their importance in reaching an outcome, either past or present, bolsters the well-being of first children. They want nothing more than to believe that their contribution is central and important to the people with whom they are involved, and they thrive on this kind of direct information.

Firt children also need to learn from others that they are important for who they are, as well as for what they do. Explicit statements that they are valued and loved, regardless of what they do, affirm first children's worth. Without statements such as "I like you," "I love you," "You're wonderful," "Just having you around is nice," first children do not realize that they are worthwhile for who they are. When others assure them that they are valued for who they are, first children do not need as much approval for what they do. The more they accept this validation that they are valuable individuals, the more they themselves can validate the worth of what they do.

First children tend to forget past accomplishments and focus on what they must do in the present. Because their self-esteem is linked to continuous productivity, and because they worry that their efforts are insufficient, first children are concerned if they are not involved in a task. It becomes a self-worth issue. They need others to remind them of their past accomplishments. They also need such reminders when they are overwhelmed by the details of a new task. In this situation, they may be asking "Why do I have to do this?" or complaining about the number of things that they have to do. Simple reminders that connect them to specific past projects seem to free them to accomplish their tasks. It is easier for first children to accept feedback about mistakes if the person who notes the error explicitly recognizes the effort with which they tried to do what they perceived as right. A simple comment, such as "I understand what you were trying to do," before a request such as "Could you try it a different way?" helps first children incorporate suggestions into their activities without becoming defensive.

When first children feel overwhelmed and helpless, become mired in detail, and are confused about the best way to succeed, they do not call for help. Instead, they build a cognitive, analytical explanation that others often interpret as irresponsibility. In these situations, first children need someone to help them explore their feelings of helplessness, confusion, and fear. If they believe that the other person is judging them or discounting their effort, they deny all feelings and argue with the other person. It is important to approach these feelings in an unpretentious way, validating their extreme effort and noting the tremendous burden that trying to solve such a complicated problem alone must be.

First children do best in structured situations. They like expectations to be clearly stated, steps in accomplishing tasks to be defined, and goals to be made explicit. Others can help by providing first children with all the information that they need.

Because first children try to enforce rules as part of their family role assignment, they worry about whether others are in compliance. With cooperation from others in following explicit rules, first children can avoid disagreements and problems. This frees them to be productive in other ways.

Tables that summarize the characteristic response patterns for first siblings are in the Appendix.

CHAPTER 5
Second-Born Siblings

In anticipation of the arrival of the second child, the parents focus inward on the family system in ways that may not be recognized by the family, but are nevertheless powerful. Psychologically and logistically, nothing is the same for the second child as for the first child. Although inexperienced as parents for the first child, the mother and father had no question about the centrality of that child. Being first gave that child a unique and indisputable place in the family. Regardless of how much the second child is wanted and loved, however, the parents are uncertain about this new family member's place in the family. For example, the parents may wonder if they can love the second child as much as they love the first, if they can decentralize their focus on the first child and make psychological room for the second child. They begin to resolve this issue with the birth of the second child, as they acknowledge their feelings for the second child. The issue before birth may be reflected in the messages received by their second child, however.

Place will never be emphasized in the same way for children that follow. Parents may wonder where to put additional children or how to take care of them financially and emotionally, but the issue of place is psychologically met and resolved with the second child.

Functional Family System Roles

As a result of the questions about their place in the family, second children lose their places easily, even though they know they are loved and accepted as family members. When new or unsettling situations arise in the family or in other contexts, second children are insecure until they determine their place. This is one of the reasons that second children feel responsible for stability in the family structure.

As second children enter the family unit, they receive a family role assignment that serves the needs and goals of individual family members, and the system as a whole. Their role assignment is complementary to the one received by first children because the needs of the system differ from those of the system at the time when the first children were born.

Job Assignments

The increase in the family system's maintenance need that results from the addition of a fourth person to a three-person system in large part determines the job assignment for second children. With first children responsible for the explicit rules of the family, the primary function of second children is to perceive and support the implicit elements in family rules and relationships. For example, affect, such as unexpressed and/or unrecognized anger in one or more family members and unstated information about events or rules, is part of the implicit structure in families. Therefore, second children detect and represent the emotional needs and wishes of others by making them an explicit part of a given context.

Implicit elements in relationships, such as expectations, feelings, and wishes of participants, clog the channels of communication. When implicit information is relevant to the interaction, the effects may cause distress in the system. For example, with the arrival of the second child, the mother may find that she cannot be as productive and efficient in some areas as she had been in the past. When the father comes home from a strenuous day at work, both children are demanding attention, the house is cluttered, and dinner is not ready. The father may be very understanding and help to relieve some of the tension by preparing dinner, playing with the first child, or holding a fussy baby. On the surface, everything appears to be fine—the father and the mother are talking about the adjustments in their lives and predicting normalcy soon. At an implicit level, however, unmet needs may be creating anger, hopelessness, fatigue, guilt, resentment, and despair in one or both of the spouses. They may not express or even recognize these thoughts and feelings. Because of this blockage in the channels of communication, information is not flowing.

By identifying with the implicit emotional needs and feelings of other family members, second children represent the unacknowledged discrepancies between the family's implicit and explicit rules and values. The existence of these discrepancies creates tension for second children and may create pain if hurt, anger, sadness, and fear are part of the implicit emotional undercurrents. The degree of tension or pain is related to the intensity of the unresolved conflict in the family system. Second children manage the tension or pain by forcing someone to make it explicit, by acting it out themselves, by distracting attention from the conflicts, by teasing, or by expressing it themselves. They are not usually aware that their feelings and behaviors are connected to the undercurrents in the family, but their role is purposeful as they identify and open clogged channels of communication.

Second children also have some responsibility for productivity needs in the family. They respond to the need for increased productivity by doing their share. They do not experience the same internal pressure for products and results that first children experience, however, because their primary focus on the need for stability leads them to monitor the quality of a given task; thus process is more important to them than is the product. Therefore, they gauge success by the quality rather than by the quantity of products. These attempts at product control yield an outcome, either completion of tasks or value, that satisfies a family or personal need or goal. Consequently, second children may sometimes appear to be focused on results in much the same way as first children are.

Interpersonal Responsibilities

Much like first children, second children expect to have a unique relationship with each family member in order to accomplish their job assignments. While first children connect to each person to ensure that everyone follows the rules of the family and to help everyone be productive, second children connect to each person to help family members make implicit messages explicit and to process the quality of performance by family members.

Because first children have already become responsible to and for one parent more than the other, second children tend to do the same with the other parent in order to balance the system. Second children form close ties with the mother when they see her as primarily responsible for the mental health and stability of the family. They learn implicitly from her what needs in the family should be expressed and the appropriate manner of their expression. Although they are not responsible for the mother's position in the family, second children are closely connected to the underlying tone that she creates.

If the mother abdicates her responsibility, is inept in some ways, or is emotionally or physically ill, the second child's job is more difficult. In these cases, the mother does not or cannot express her feelings. Consistently, she is even unaware of her unresolved issues, especially those that involve her husband and family of origin. Second children unknowingly fight the mother's battles and harass everyone in an effort to clear the undercurrents. Because second children do not realize that they are acting out their mother's concerns, they often feel "crazy" and "bad." Moreover, others have difficulty understanding their behavior.

Social Interactions

First and second children interact with both parents, but their role assignments qualify their interactions in some ways. For example, first children look at the mother through the father, while second children look at the father through the mother. One result of this phenomenon is that the relationship between first and second siblings mirrors the marriage of their parents.

In interacting with others, second children are often tender, sensitive, and caring. At times, they act directly on their intuitions and feelings. When tuned into the other person and focused on that person's feelings, they are wonderful listeners. At other times, they are rational, distant, and goal-oriented, with all their attention focused on a task to be finished. The fact that they switch back and forth between these modes of interaction can be very disconcerting for others. When second children become emotionally distant, they completely shut out people who are interacting with them. Family members and friends experience confusion when they are suddenly excluded. Often, second children are equally confused when they try to process what happened. They are not aware of shutting out other people and, because that is not their intention, they take no responsibility for it. This is one reason that it is difficult to confront second siblings.

Unless they receive specific instruction about boundaries from their parents and others, second children do not realize that they have a right to establish boundaries in areas of their own lives. Furthermore, they are often quite unaware of the personal boundaries of others. This failure to recognize boundaries may cause them difficulty in social interaction. For example, they can be inappropriate in the questions they ask, in the information they give, and in their physical and emotional closeness to others.

Second children often appear to be at odds with first children for a number of reasons. They may be engaged in a legitimate power struggle, in a typical rivalry issue, or simply in the process of doing their jobs. More than one of these elements may be involved in the same situation. First children hierarchically have more power in the sibling subsystem because initially they are physically stronger. Also, parents require first children to do certain things for their younger siblings. This phenomenon of hierarchy is normal and occurs throughout the sibling subsystem. The age or physical strength of the older sibling almost always creates conflict interpersonally, however. Because their role assignments are complementary, it may be expected that first and second children will cooperate when assigned to the same job. Their differences in perceptions may create conflict, however. First children focus on getting the job finished in order to move on to the next task. Second children focus on doing the task properly. Furthermore, the second children's response to unexpressed emotional pain, anger, or indifference to the participants in the task may block progress on the task for first children. For example, because first children may not express their underlying feelings of fear and anxiety about the performance of the task, second children may focus on the emotional undercurrents and become obstinate, refusing to do what is expected.

Conflict may also arise because second children often tell their parents when first children do not conform to explicit rules, thus making an implicit statement. Although it may appear that second children are eager to cause trouble for first children with one or both parents, second children may only be doing their job assignment by pointing out discrepancies between the explicit and the implicit. Consequently, second children "boss" others in the family in an attempt to get them to follow family rules. When communication is open and family members do what they say they will do, there are fewer emotional undercurrents. In these circumstances, second children do not need to "tell tales" about anyone, to anyone. They may be engaged in a legitimate power struggle, in a typical rivalry issue, simply in the process of doing their jobs. More than one of these elements may be involved in the same situation.

Second children can live totally for someone else or they can be totally independent. In the former case, they do not assert their wishes, and their identity merges with that of the other person; they are unable to separate their feelings from those of the other person or to recognize boundaries between them. Their very existence is devoted to taking care of the other person, and they lose their separateness. This type of interaction and melding is not within their explicit, cognitive awareness. When second children are able to discern their own boundaries, they can assert themselves and make demands, and they can simultaneously help and support another person.

Perceptual Orientation

Focus and Awareness

Second children focus more on implicit messages, affect, and process than they do on content. They pick up subtle messages that are not usually noticed by others, sensing symbolic and imaginative meanings of reality and of the underlying structure of a situation. They are also aware of explicit family rules and values. Their understanding of the underlying structure allows second children to process events and to judge the quality of performance.

Like first children, second children tend to focus on details rather than on the total picture. One of the reasons for this is that they were born into a family with only four people. When they focus on the literal aspects of phenomena, they are logical and analytical in order to understand the parts. Consequently, the focus for both first and second children is primarily on individuals and small subsystems rather than on the system as a whole.

Cognitive Patterns

Second children perceive issues in terms of polarities. As mentioned earlier, they fluctuate between an affective and a cognitive stance. To them, affect and cognition provide two streams of information, both of which can occur at explicit and implicit levels. Second children sometimes have trouble integrating the two streams of information at the two different levels, and they choose one over the other by polarizing. Polarities are most evident when the distance between explicit family rules and implicit family rules is so great that second children are overwhelmed by the incongruities.

The polarization can result in a restrictive and distorted picture of reality, as the transitions or connecting links between the two poles are missing. Second children are not always aware of the missing pieces; consequently, they sometimes act as if something is complete when it is not. To obtain complete data, they must consistently work for integration of affect and cognition. Second children sometimes refuse to consider new data, however, as if new information would upset an internal balance of some kind and create more pain. Sometimes, they appear to be overwhelmed by implicit information and unable to accept additional explicit information.

Second children assume that everyone knows and senses what they know and sense. If no one else mentions the same thoughts or feelings, second children assume that no one else is aware of them and that these thoughts and feelings are not important enough to discuss. Second children also assume that if they think something or feel something it has been made explicit. Because of these assumptions, second children often believe that they have communicated information when they have not.

Even though both first children and second children focus on parts, their cognitive patterns are different. Whereas first children seek explanations based on the meaning of separate parts, second children focus on parts in order to understand the underlying structure (i.e., implicit emotional waves, unexpressed cognitive processes, beliefs, expectations, and images). Although second children sense underlying structure, it is not always in their awareness;

they constantly strive to discern implicit structure by making covert rules and information explicit.

Second children create images to understand their experiences. These images are usually quite visual and it is easy for second children to describe them in metaphoric and imagery language. For example, an adult second sibling was asked to close her eyes and imagine a receptacle in which she could place all her feelings. Without hesitation, she chose a wooden bucket and then immediately changed it to a large copper washtub, stating that the bucket was too small. When asked to identify one feeling at a time, describe it, and put it in the tub, she easily did so. Her descriptions were vivid in the color, size, shape, weight, and texture of each feeling. Her hands held each feeling as she described it and placed it in the tub.

Affective Patterns

Second children sense and collect other people's feelings and tensions as if they were their own. It is difficult for most second children to identify, label, and sort out their own feelings, because their feelings seem to meld (i.e., blend or fuse) with the affect of others. In this process, second children lose part of their identity and have little awareness of their own boundaries. Although the attachments of first children never take on the quality of melding and blending their identities with those of other people, the melding process is an important affective pattern for second children.

Second children take on the pain of other people through the melding process. Depending on the magnitude of the pain, they become frightened, breathe very shallowly, or even hold their breath. These actions indicate intense, implicit emotional undercurrents. Second children often do not cognitively know that the pain is there, but they meld with it. Unless someone points it out to them or the person with the pain expresses it, second children seldom see the degree to which they are taking care of someone else's symptomatic behavior. This is part of the melding pattern.

Second children may try to get away from someone else's pain and stress, but their behavior may appear unruly, crazy, or incongruent. To observers, the problem seems to belong to the second children, but it becomes clear under examination that their behavior is intended to help the other person. For example, if the mother is so highly stressed that she is not performing normally, her second child may panic and behave in chaotic and disruptive ways. Small children may cry, scream, throw tantrums, and cling to adults to distract or force an admission of the mother's pain. As adults, second siblings may harass others, disrupt others' routines, get sick, or threaten to leave. Second siblings are usually unaware that they take on someone else's burdens and symptoms in order to force an expression of the pain. This behavior puzzles others, because people who are not second children are usually unaware of implicit pain and stress in family systems.

There are two processes in which the flooding of emotion incapacitates second children. In one, the intensity of the implicit emotional undercurrents and the incongruence between explicit behavior and emotion in a specific context overwhelm the second children as they meld with the unacknowledged feelings, of others in the system. In the other, the tensions and feelings accumulate over a period of time from a number of interpersonal interactions, and second children unexpectedly become saturated with emotional debris when they move into a situation that has a low level of emotional undercurrents. Second children are confused and surprised when this happens. Others are distracted by the behavior of the second children, because it does not match the circumstances.

Second children who are flooded with emotion behave in one of two ways. They may feel out of control and act irrationally by changing the subject several times in a conversation, picking fights for no apparent reason, or being unreasonably emotional. On the other hand, they may polarize their experience, organizing it cognitively or affectively. They must either shut it all out or deal with it all. If they are affective, they begin to talk about their emotions; if they are cognitive, they artificially separate themselves from the emotion and distance themselves from others.

Second children also polarize their feelings when they are overwhelmed with the intensity of the messages that they are receiving. They can be happy one moment and sad the next, giddy and silly one moment and content the next. In relationships, they can be overly close or distant. Because the movement between emotional polarities is more evident, observers tend to think that affect is more important to second children than cognition is; however, this is not true. Second children alternate between cognitive and affective polarities in order to integrate the middle to make sense and order of their world. When overwhelmed by the intensity of the cognitive and affective levels to which they are attending, second children have difficulty integrating the middle.

Polarized, cognitive second children seem to be totally out of touch with feelings. In most situations, they ignore others' feelings and deny their own. More men than women are polarized cognitively, possibly because they are influenced by societal standards for males. When polarized, cognitive second children do become aware of their feelings; they usually must deal with a great deal of previously unidentified pain.

As a result of their cognitive-affective patterns, second children tend to make assumptions quickly and to act on these assumptions as if there were no chance for error. Second children trust their assumptions which are based on what they sense in the implicit structure of a situation, because their intuition has frequently been verified in the past when the implicit was made explicit. Because they are often "right," they tend to believe that they are always right. Consequently, they may appear to others as presumptuous, arrogant, and intrusive when they act on their assumptions, especially if their assumptions are related to others' feelings. When someone challenges their assumptions, they are surprised; usually, however, they are willing to amend their position if they are not too threatened by the situation.

Identity and Sense of Well-Being

Self-Esteem and Well-Being

Like any other child, the second child needs to have a sense of uniqueness and to be valued as an individual. When second children recognize and admit their own feelings, they can stand on their own, work to meet their own needs, and accept their own uniqueness. Second children learn to sort out their own feelings when family members, especially the mother, admit their feelings. Even when family members admit their feelings, however, they never admit them all. Consequently, second children may have difficulty with identity and sense of well-being.

The main identity issue for second children is "Do I have a place?" The need to be unique is heightened by the further identity issue of "What is my place?" An explicit, acknowledged personal place gives second children a sense of security. Every time they meld with someone, are flooded with emotions, feel overwhelmed by the tension and pain in situations, or enter a new situation, they temporarily lose their place. Although new environments may be similar to previous ones, second children are cautious and watchful as they determine if there is a place for them. A simple thing like inadvertently setting the dinner table one place short can be very upsetting if a second child is the last one to come to the table. A change of school is difficult for most children, but every new setting is a trial for second children. The sooner they have their own desk, room, and teacher, the more secure they are. Social situations are very stressful until some meaningful relationships can be formed.

Second children derive their identities from filling the emotional gaps in the family, or at least from being in tune with the underlying feelings of others. They tend to feel and act as though they are extensions of other people; their sense of joy, sorrow, and failure depends totally on the experience of others. Consequently, they have difficulty maintaining a separate identity. In order to be functional, however, second children need to recognize their differentness from others. Because second children learn early to meld with their mother's feelings, needs, and wishes through their functional family role assignment to her, it is particularly difficult for them to establish a clear identity that is separate from that of their mother.

Before they can have separate identities, second children must clearly identify their boundaries—emotionally, intellectually, and physically. In doing this, they become self-sufficient and purposeful. With assurance from their parents and siblings that they do have a separate, unique place and that they make important contributions to the family, they can establish their own identities.

Threats to Well-Being

Second children are psychologically threatened when they lose their sense of having a unique, separate place, and their sense of being a separate self. They feel threatened when people deny their own feelings, making the explicit and implicit incongruent. This is particularly true if the denial occurs after second children have attempted to make their intuitive assumptions explicit. By denying their feelings, these other people deny the second child's reality.

Second children feel threatened when they are flooded by so many emotions that they cannot sort these feelings logically, and make connections between the cognitive and affective parts. In interpersonal situations, others often understand the connections and expect second children to understand them too. Although they sense at an implicit level that something is expected of them, they do not know what to do; therefore, they polarize even more. Consequently, second children feel threatened by an interpersonal event that does not make sense to them.

Responses to Threats to Well-Being

It is not easy to determine when second children feel threatened, because they often do not realize it themselves. This is true for both children and adults. Generally, they look and feel exhausted emotionally. They use indirect maneuvers that are distracting in order to smooth things over, or they may withdraw.

Outwardly, they react to incongruous situations by waiting helplessly for someone to clarify the discrepancies. They can appear obstinate when they are afraid because they do not know what is happening. In this case, they often become uncooperative, refusing to give information. Their behavior becomes rebellious, they break rules, get into fights, challenge authority, withdraw, and run away. Highly intellectual or highly emotional, they appear uninvolved and remote; overly involved and helpless; or aimless. They may present elaborate rational explanations and adhere to them tenaciously. It may appear that they are listening to new information, but it is likely that—because they feel threatened—they are blocking information rather than denying it.

Siblings' Needs from Others

The family system generally, and individual family members specifically, can provide most of what second siblings need from others. When second siblings do not feel threatened, they can deal with rejection and nonacceptance much like anyone else. When they feel threatened, however, they need clear acceptance as a person, recognition of their need for a place, and reminders of the uniqueness of that place.

Because of their behavior when they feel threatened (e.g., tantrums, hitting, yelling, name calling, and rebelliousness), others may want to reject second children at this time. Yet, it is precisely then that they need direct assurance. No family is consistent with this kind of assurance; even if they receive this assurance only intermittently, however, second siblings can recover from temporary "loss of place" and feelings of rejection. When parents can stay close physically and assure second siblings that they are always a part of the family, regardless of how bad their behavior, the psychological threat decreases. Then the consequences of their inappropriate behavior can be explained to them by the parents or others.

When second siblings are overwhelmed by the emotional debris that they have collected from others, they need to have people admit their feelings, needs, and expectations. They also need other people to clarify their own boundaries so that they can learn to do the same. Second siblings need to be reminded that it is appropriate for them to have boundaries and to establish their own rules about these boundaries.

Tables that summarize the characteristic response patterns for second siblings are in the Appendix.

CHAPTER 6

Third-Born Siblings

When the third child enters the family, the structure and organization of the family are much more complex than they were when either the first or the second child was born. Third children do not have the benefit of watching relationships develop; they are thrown into a complex system of existing alliances and relationships. The older two children have formed reference points to the father and the mother, respectively, with the first child focused on explicit information and the second focused on implicit structure. Because third children are always exposed to established relationships (e.g., the marriage, relationships between parents and other brothers or sisters, and relationships between other siblings), they have fewer opportunities to develop one-on-one relationships in the family than do the first two children. Thus, the presence of a third child leads to the development of many triangle subsystems in the family.

Functional Family System Roles

The stability needs of the family system increase greatly with the addition of the third child. The parents focus on trying to balance the demands of the family and meet everyone's needs as each dyadic relationship structure adjusts to include this third person.

Job Assignments

Third children are assigned the task of keeping the balance in dyadic relationships in the family. In doing so, third children not only find a unique way of belonging to the family, but also help the family cope with the increased complexity of the system and meet some of its stability needs.

Third children become especially responsible for balance in the marital relationship, because it is the most important and explicit of the dyads in the family. It is explicit in the sense that the roles of husband and wife have personal and societal expectations attached. Being observers of dyadic dynamics from their birth, third children discover rules about the appropriate degree of closeness, conflict, dependency, intrusiveness, and loyalty in the marriage. Their identity and behavior literally reflects the underlying interaction between their parents. They feel responsible for the dynamics and quality of the marital relationship.

Several weeks after a family therapy session, a third sibling described how responsible he felt for his parents' marriage and what he did differently after the session:

> Before therapy, the one thing I did was sort of always listen in as I hung around in the background. Like I'd be up in my room and they'd be arguing, and instead of, you know, being with them in the room to listen to them argue, I'd sort of listen in from my bedroom. I would listen in and I'd get a full scoop, as much as I could. And then it hurt me a lot. Our therapist told me that I didn't need to do that for them. I think I did it a little after that, but I never . . . if they are fighting I just go back to what I am doing. I don't hide from them, but I'm not listening in . . . . That's one thing I did learn and it's helped me a lot, a real lot . . . . That is probably the best thing that came out of that session for me.

Another third sibling described how she took care of relationships in her family:

> There was a lot of confrontation between my sister and my mom, and I stuck up for both of them because . . . well, I could see Anna's point, but I disagreed with her. I wish all of them would talk to my grandma. I get along fine with her now, and I wish they all would. I know she talks a lot, but she is lonely. To me, it seems like they think it is so much a sacrifice to talk to my dad and my grandma. This situation seemed like it was a lot of hurt for me, but not for anyone else.

Third children also identify family relationship issues, although they may appear to be uninvolved in family interactions. If asked in a safe context, however, third children can describe the issues with which relationships are struggling. Thus, not only do third children seek to enforce relationship rules in the family, but also they try to facilitate connections between other family members. By doing so, they restore balance and harmony to the dyads.

Interpersonal Responsibilities

Third children are nonparticipant negotiators within the family. They seek to clarify the contexts in which dyads occur, and they move in and out of relationships with each member of the dyad in order to give support. For example, they may appear to side with one parent at times, but they soon move out of that alliance and support the other. Even when they overtly support one parent, they covertly support the other parent in some way. They also do this with siblings and friends.

Third children can tolerate and at times even prefer ambiguity in their position with each party. They feel that, if they were to take a position with one side or the other, they would disrupt the ongoing relationships and create disharmony. Therefore, they may be content to identify the issue rather than to support either side. At other times, however, they deliberately form an alliance with one side to imbalance the relationship. Third children see both of these strategies as ways of fulfilling their job assignment (i.e., helping dyads to deal with interaction issues). If third children fail to facilitate negotiation between the two parties involved, they create some problem that will draw the other two together to focus on the difficulty created. Of course, this all occurs at an implicit level, usually beyond awareness of the third child.

Feeling a responsibility for the marital relationship, third children seek to maintain balance in the marriage by connecting to both the mother and the father. If they are connected to one parent and not the other, they pull back to try to make connections with the other parent as well. They learn early in infancy not to stay consistently connected with one person in a family relationship for too long without also connecting to the other person in that relationship.

In dysfunctional families, third children feel personally responsible for the problems in relationships. They feel that the marriage and other relationships would improve if they, as third children, were better people. In such cases, third children do everything in their power to restore balance and stability to the marriage. If failure is imminent and the pain too great, third children become withdrawn and isolated from other family members.

Social Interactions

Third children identify with and support dyadic relationships in their families of origin, and of course, they continue to do this in other relationships as well. In fact, third children seem to carry their parents' marital relationship rules and issues into any dyadic relationship that they form. For example, if the parents have good communication in their marriage, the third child can be close in dyadic relationships. If the parents feel that their marriage is special, the third child feels special and worthwhile as a person. If the parents' marital relationship is poor and the conflict is chronic with no resolution, however, the third child has difficulty forming close dyadic relationships without therapeutic intervention because the child has learned dysfunctional relationship principles.

Although third children are comfortable with people and may have good social skills, they form in-depth relationships with other people slowly and cautiously. They hold back in relationships until they know exactly where they stand with the other person. The issue is one of trust; third children have such a strong need to be separate that it makes them seem reluctant and distrustful. Once committed to a relationship, however, third children find it difficult to disconnect and will do anything necessary to stay in the relationship.

In relating to others, third children are intensely involved in the system to help maintain relationships, but they also must detach themselves in order to meet their need for a separate identity. Freedom to be independent in relationships is very important to third children. If they feel trapped or confined, they fight to free themselves. Because of third children's efforts to keep their choices open, others often find them ambivalent. Third children appear to be warm, caring, and involved one minute and totally detached in the next. They are physically present, but they have retreated emotionally and psychologically to some distant, inner sanctum. Because of this process, others often see third children as contradictory, inconsistent, and incongruent. Third children are usually surprised when they receive such feedback from other people, because they see themselves as involved, connected, and caring.

This capacity to be in and out of relationships gives third children power in social interactions. They learn as infants, often at the implicit level, that their behavior in triadic relationships affects the interaction dynamics of the relationship between the other two people. Whether they work for balance or whether they disrupt the ongoing status quo of the other relationship in the triangle, they sense the impact of their behavior. This process teaches them that they are powerful. Third children do not necessarily seek power; rather, it is a byproduct of their assignment to balance relationships.

When conflict is present in a relationship, third children often withdraw, physically or emotionally, to resolve the issues in their own mind. Because they focus on issues rather than on feelings and because they can usually see both sides of an issue, problem solving becomes a matter of analyzing and weighing data rather than a dyadic communication process. The other person in the relationship is usually frustrated when the third child returns after a conflict and announces that all is resolved. The other person has been waiting for communication channels to open and feelings to be resolved, but the third child can resolve the conflict alone because of the third child's focus on issues. Third children often have difficulty understanding their partner's feelings about this process.

Finally, third children usually like to do things with other people. So much of their family role is associated with dyadic interaction that they are more comfortable if at least two people are involved in an activity. "Can I take a friend along?" is a frequent question of third children.

Perceptual Orientation

Focus and Awareness

The major focus of the family at the birth of the third child is inward to relationships within the family because the increase in the number of dyads and triads creates more possibilities for instability in the family. The family system requires additional maintenance as unmet goals for individuals and dyadic subsystems accumulate and disrupt the system. As a result of the family focus, third children are focused on relationships and feel threatened when relationships are not going well for family members.

To third children, the world is a place full of connections; therefore, they search for connections and correlations between individual parts in the world. Their perceptual orientation develops as a result of their constant involvement and identity in family triads. They examine the ways in which things harmonize, contrast, and work together. Although aware of the context in which things occur, they sometimes fail to observe details and parts. They are concerned with how things are connected and how they operate, rather than purpose.

Third children focus on issues in relationships. They look at ways in which participants agree in relationships and ways in which they disagree. They examine the context of the situation, because the context contains the underlying principles that predict the occurrence of the same event at another time. In relationships, third children are more aware of the dynamics of interaction and the implications for the relationship than the details of ideas or the feelings and implicit needs of individuals.

Cognitive Patterns

Third children are not nearly as interested in parts and pieces of information as they are in how the pieces work together. By connecting enough parts, third siblings have a sense of the whole. They are interested in the process by which they reach answers. They have little concern about the answer itself (the what) if they cannot understand the process (the how) by which the answer was derived. Third children need to know that given a similar context, they can reach the answer by means of the same process at another time. If the process is transferable to a whole set of other contexts, mastering the underlying principles of that process gives third children great satisfaction.

Their ability to understand underlying principles and connections allows third children to search for new ways in which parts can be connected. They are superstars at reorganizing information to illustrate how the parts mesh together and contrast, but they usually miss the details of the parts themselves, particularly when the details are not related to the connections between parts. They sometimes limit the context prematurely by omitting details and parts. Third children can also make the mistake of leaving people out of contexts and issues, because people are individual parts of these contexts and issues. Third children are quite surprised when this is pointed out to them.

Affective Patterns

Third children feel deeply and are sensitive, caring individuals. They sometimes appear apathetic, however, particularly if they have stepped away from a relationship for a moment to resolve some issue. Although third children may appear happy and secure, acting as if everything is under control, appearances are sometimes deceptive. Beneath the image is an intensely emotional person who has retreated psychologically to determine how the pieces of an issue fit together. Such distancing is a survival mechanism that helps third children maintain an identity.

Healthy third children can identify feelings if they make the effort to focus affectively rather than only cognitively on the issues. They can express their own feelings very clearly when they see their feelings as relevant to a clarification of the context. If third children are not focused on feelings when others want them to be, those with whom they interact must legitimize feelings as part of the context of the relationship. When this occurs, third children are very attentive to other people's feelings.

Identity and Sense of Well-Being

The identity and sense of well-being for third children are very much connected to the kind of family interaction and family needs that exist when they are born. Their solid identity and sense of well-being are derived from the successful functioning of family dyads, particularly the marriage, and the fulfillment of their role in relation to those family relationships.

Self-Esteem and Well-Being

For third children, self-esteem is very much connected to the stability of the marital relationship. It is also influenced by the way their parents feel about them. Third children want to know where they stand with other people, and it is especially important to them to know how each of their parents feels about them. The security of knowing that both parents love and accept them, regardless of what they do, enhances the well-being of third children.

Well-being in third children is also dependent on their ability to discover rules of relationships and the underlying principles of all processes. They feel secure when they can identify the ways in which things work, and make them work. By ensuring that each piece is in its proper place in relationship to every other part, they clarify the context of any situation, which contributes to their sense of well-being. They feel good when they show others how to get from one point to the next and provide new perspectives.

To third children, choices represent personal security. Their desire to keep choices open appears to come from their focus on balancing relationships. They could form a coalition with either parent, but they maintain family balance by not choosing either, at least not for very long. Because perceptual orientation and identity are heavily influenced by this kind of family interaction, third children's sense of well-being appears to require the availability of choices.

Threats to Well-Being

When their choices are taken away, third children rebel and take either a fight or flight stance. Third children can decide to choose on their own, but they become very angry when someone else forces them to make a choice. Not only may a forced choice disrupt a carefully maintained balance, but also it may eliminate all other alternatives, both of which are distressing to third children. Everyone finds it difficult or awkward to make choices in some situations, but the pressure for third children is connected to their identity and sense of well-being. To be put in a position without choices is unbearable for third children.

Third children also feel threatened when there is unresolved conflict within dyadic relationships in the family. When the basic core of a dyadic relationship is poor, third children suffer and feel that they are to blame in some mystical way. For example, when marital partners lack commitment, when one or both spouses are not working to better the marriage, and when the tension is not openly admitted and discussed, third children suffer. Under such circumstances, they are likely to be the identified patients in therapy. If family members can admit that there is conflict and have the skills to resolve the tension, however, the third child is fine.

Responses to Threats to Well-Being

When they have no choices, third children feel confined and trapped. It is not making the choice that is important; it is having the choice. The lack of choices becomes an issue of freedom to third children, and they fight relentlessly either to have their choices restored or to escape from the situation.

Third children's responses to threatening events take on a number of different appearances. At times, they may appear to be uninvolved, uncaring, and indifferent. Others may describe them as apathetic. In actuality, however, they have disappeared into introspection to study the issues. They are overwhelmed if they must remain psychologically available, but this retreat to an inner psychological place that they create inside of themselves allows them to rest.

At other times, third children appear ambivalent and unwilling to commit themselves to a choice. They may waver back and forth, with their current position dependent on the most recent input from other people. Just as they move in and out of relationships, they move in and out of the decision-making process. As a result, they often appear to be on the periphery of things, but they feel less threatened. Moreover, they are seldom as uninvolved as they appear. Although they are not experts on the individual members of the family, they understand better than does anyone else how the family members connect with each other. They can immediately pinpoint all the relationship issues and describe the workings of the family and its subsystems.

Siblings' Needs from Others

Third children fear being disconnected from other people. They need other people to provide reassurance by expressing both the positive and negative aspects about the connections of third children to them. Third children want to know such things as whether what they do is of value to the other person, whether the other person likes them, and whether they can trust the other person.

Third children need to know that they are appreciated, not so much for what they do, but for their presence. Their need for appreciation stems from their focus on balance in relationships. Messages of appreciation about their presence help them feel that it is the balancing force in relationships and that they are succeeding in their role to bring about this balance. By accepting the right of third children to have choices and by allowing them the freedom not to make a choice, other people can legitimize their need to have choices. Other people can also help third children by creating choices to provide alternatives. Finally, others can help by not pushing them to make a choice, to act on a decision that someone else made for them, or to make a decision that affects other people. If they feel pushed, another's investment in their welfare, loving kindness, and request for a decision for their own good have no more impact than a dictatorial and uncaring approach would have. Under these circumstances, third children need to be left alone.

When third children are troubled, they need to be reminded that they are not alone, that others are connected to them, and that their context can be broadened to include other people, if necessary. This allows them to accept help from others in solving their problems. Sometimes, by going away, third children leave those who should be involved in choosing and making decisions out of the context. No one can force third children to stay psychologically available, but they need to know that they will still have connections when they return.

Acceptance of third children's in-and-out behavior helps them feel understood and connected. They need to be independent and have permission to operate from a detached position. Third children need to have a place to go and be themselves. Although this can be a physical place, a psychological place is far more important. Going to this place sometimes gives them rest; at other times, it gives them a chance to sort through pain or anger and seek their own solutions. Although this retreat makes them psychologically unavailable to others for a short time, they always return if given the freedom to go away.

Finally, third children need to feel trust in relationships. They proceed slowly and cautiously until they are sure that the other person can be trusted. They need to know that their connection to the other person will continue, even if they go away. When that trust has been established, they are committed to the relationship.

Tables that summarize the characteristic response patterns for third siblings are in the Appendix.

CHAPTER 7

Fourth-Born Siblings

The system becomes extremely complex when the fourth child enters the family. The integration of the personal needs of six individuals with the productivity and stability needs of the family requires clear family purposes and goals. The major goal of the family system is to meet the needs of all individuals and the needs of a much more complex family system, while maintaining unity and harmony.

Functional Family System Roles

From infancy, fourth children respond to the increased complexity in the family system by accepting responsibility for family unity and harmony so that family purposes remain clear and goals can be met. They survey the whole family and observe the movements of every family member.

Job Assignments

When fourth children enter the family, they receive the message that their job is to maintain the family system and keep it in harmony. For example, a 13-year-old fourth child described her response to the whole family during the first ten minutes of a family session. Her parents and three brothers, Eddie, 15 years old; Sam, 19 years old; and Alan, 21 years old, were also in the session.

I was so nervous. I watched Eddie, and my mom, and my mom looked so uncomfortable and Eddie was . . . . I've never known him to look so . . . he was just so tight. And I was picking up everybody's nerves and I was . . . I . . . I . . . . When I first came in there and sat down . . . cuz then it all came right at me and I . . . not only did I have my own nervousness, but I had, you know, five other people's.

This girl's account shows how fourth children survey the field and note the pain in the family. In order to fulfill their role, fourth children try to determine whether all family members are working together and if family goals are being met. The goals of individuals are important to the fourth child's role assignment only in that they are part of the larger picture. If family goals are not met, fourth children feel that they are to blame, because the family does not then have wholeness and harmony. Thus, fourth children seek to preserve the integrity of the entire system.

One of the primary duties of fourth children is to be a trouble-shooter for their family system. They do their share of work for products and results, but trouble-shooting is their more important role. They perform this role by signaling when and where there is a breakdown in the system. They are generally the first to know when there is pain in the system, and they go directly to the individual with the pain and try to make it better. Because the pain prevents the family from achieving its goals, the fourth child tries to minimize the disruption and keep the family moving toward its goals.

When the level of unity in the family is extremely low, the fourth child is likely to behave aggressively as a means of focusing the family's attention on a common problem. They may become hysterical, throw a tantrum, or grow excessively cautious. By creating a family crisis, they relieve or shift some of the tension and pain in the system and get the family working together, at the very least. This is an attempt to "fix" the family system.

Interpersonal Responsibilities

More than any other child, fourth siblings feel responsible for the family unit as a whole. Although they feel a much greater responsibility to the group, they also connect with each family member. They take care of individuals who are in pain, whether they like those individuals or not, because they feel a duty to diminish the pain in the system in order to repair the disrupted system. In distressful and disruptive moments, fourth children often move about the family, telling family members that they love them and that everything will be all right.

Fourth children feel a duty to their parents to ensure harmony in the family. When fourth children are born into the family, the parents are focused on the whole family; they are wondering how they can keep things running smoothly with so many people in the family. Therefore, fourth children receive a message that they need to help the parents accomplish this goal. This sense of duty is evident even after the parents die. Because of their perception that their parents want the family to continue to be harmonious, fourth siblings often take on additional burdens in the family after the deaths of the parents. Fourth children do not usually realize their motivations for doing this, however.

Social Interactions

Characteristically, fourth children are skillful in interacting with others and helping others feel at ease in social situations. They are highly demonstrative and impulsive in the expression of feelings (e.g., warmth and closeness) and ideas. Their impulsiveness is related to their perceptual orientation toward immediate, holistic responses to social situations.

If the family is functioning well and tensions are at a minimum, the relationships of fourth children with other family members are generally pleasant. The same is true for other social systems in which fourth children are involved, as they seem to form relationships freely and quickly. People enjoy having them around, because they are spontaneous and willing to participate in activities. The fact that they usually mix easily with groups and are comfortable with them makes sense, as they were born into a "crowd" and live with interpersonal interactions all around them. Because of the ease with which fourth children form relationships and begin care-giving behaviors, however, friends tend to think that their friendship is more important to fourth children than it really is. When friends want more than fourth children intend to give and tension builds, fourth children become very confused and feel no responsibility for the tension. Then they seem not to care at all.

As part of their pattern in social interaction, fourth children take on the tensions and stress of individuals to relieve the tension in relationships. By eliminating disruptions and restoring harmony in systems, they take care of individuals, relationships, and groups. Their care-giving behavior includes such things as touches and statements of love, pats and verbal expressions that everything will be all right, silliness, and playful antics. They tend to over-dramatize as a way to draw members of systems together to solve the problem. Minor illnesses become major crises, and a little argument becomes a holocaust.

As emotional "garbage collectors" in systems, fourth children collect information and pain that is distributed throughout the family. When the cumulative pain in the system is too great, the relationships of fourth children with others become somewhat superficial. Although they have intimate relationships with family members on occasion, this superficiality is used as a way of putting distance between themselves and the unbearable pain in a given situation. In chronically dysfunctional families, relationships of fourth children with family members are likely to be superficial all the time.

Being the smallest and newest in the family, fourth children have little power. Because of the information they collect about the family, however, they wield considerable influence. It takes the strength and resources of all members to keep the family working toward common goals; consequently, fourth children are very aware of systems, power, and responsibility. Thus, they become system experts who make significant contributions to the family's planning, implementing, and finishing the product.

In groups, fourth children generally prefer either a democratic structure or one in which there is an explicit balance of power and responsibility. They support power positions if the person in authority is competent, fair, and responsible. If not, they sabotage and undermine that person's position. Because they see themselves as having little personal power, but considerable potential influence, they usually prefer to be loyal lieutenants rather than leaders. If they do have the leadership role, they are likely to develop a very democratic method for governing the group. Often without expecting any personal reward, they hope to help a group establish objectives and work toward them. They are willing to accept added responsibilities in the group if they clearly perceive the connection of such responsibilities to the growth and welfare of the organization as a whole, and if they are assured of sufficient support to keep the extra responsibility from adding substantially to their personal burden.

Generally, fourth children are very supportive of their parents, especially of the parent who makes and implements specific decisions. If the parent who has power to make decisions refuses to do so, thereby forcing others to make the decisions, fourth children tend to undermine and sabotage that parent. This situation is difficult for fourth children, however, because they are responsible for harmony in the family. Their nonsupport of that parent can take the form of rebellious behavior, harassment of the parents, or withdrawal.

The reward sought by most fourth children in relationships is an acknowledgment that their effort or their friendship leads to some improvement in the system or in the individual as a member of the system. If there is little or no indication of such progress over time, fourth children terminate relationships rather abruptly and for no apparent reason; conversely, they often maintain a relationship that is unsatisfactory to them when the other person needs it and uses it productively.

Perceptual Orientation

The world that confronts fourth children is very large and very complex. Their perceptual orientation originates in the way that they view the family as they serve it and are served by it. Like their siblings, they focus on certain aspects of their environment and develop specific beliefs and habits of perception that form interactive cognitive and affective patterns.

Focus and Awareness

With the birth of the fourth child, family members focus both inward and outward—inward to meet stability and productivity needs in the family, and outward to manage children and family through changing developmental stages. More family members are interacting with societal units that serve the family and its members such as work environments, schools, churches, friends, and age-specific activities (e.g., Little League, performance groups, Cub Scouts, church groups). The best way to keep the family functioning smoothly and meet everyone's needs is the question of paramount concern. As a result of this focus, fourth children are very aware of the needs of the entire family and their responsibility for helping the family to be happy and productive.

Fourth children focus on the whole field, the Gestalt, and on the beginning, middle, and end of tasks as part of the Gestalt. Purposeful behaviors in the entire family that move the family toward some end are also part of their focus. As they perceptually form the Gestalt, they are aware of both explicit and implicit information. This reading of the system helps them in their functional role of preserving the integrity of the system with unity and harmony.

Cognitive Patterns

Fourth children have a good grasp on the Gestalt as they experience first the whole and only then the manner in which the parts work together. If possible, they first anticipate the conclusions, then identify and arrange the specific issues or pieces accordingly.

While their perceptions encompass a wide sphere, fourth children summarize experience superficially, prematurely, and often dramatically. Their perceptions of Gestalts take the form of "circular wholes" that appear to be complete, but the circles are usually closed prematurely. They learn to draw the circles quickly so that they will not be completely overwhelmed by the burdens of the whole family. As a result, their perceptions may be accurate, but they exclude relevant pieces of information. Their total confidence in the accuracy of their perceptions disregards the superficiality used to form the conclusions and is sometimes interpreted as arrogance. Unless, however, they are highly threatened, fourth children will reexamine their conclusions when asked to do so.

Fourth children accept new information only if it can be integrated into the whole. If it cannot be integrated, it becomes burdensome to them, not only because they see the new information as disruptive to the whole, but also because they take care of the person who is giving the information by trying to deal with it, even though they see it as irrelevant. Further explanations do not help, because then the explanations become part of the burden. When this happens, fourth children become stubborn and confused.

Affective Patterns

Fourth children are often impulsive and demonstrative in dealing with their feelings. Their sensitivity to the feelings of others is also easily demonstrated. Although they sometimes collect the feelings of others as a burden, rarely are they confused about whose feelings they are.

When an adolescent fourth sibling, Tom, described his experiences in a previous therapy session, he showed how fourth children identify and describe their feelings, how they take care of others' feelings, and how they make their own interpretation of what the feelings mean.

> I felt really hopeless, and I was just sitting there watching Mike [third sibling], and I got everything from him. . . . I just got so upset. I made his problem mine, and I just sat there with my chest very tight, saying I can't cry. I can't cry. And when he said, "I just don't care anymore about the family. Now I live just for me," I was so angry. I wanted to shout, "That's my line! You can't touch it! It's not yours. It doesn't fit you." . . . And I was sitting there taking care of Mom because she was crying and trying to take care of Mike. . . . I have a habit of taking care of her feelings, and pretty much everybody else's when I feel like it. But sometimes when I don't feel like it, I get mad and tell myself that I don't really care.

Seeing the oldest brother, 25 years old, scared and upset, Tom described his reactions:

> Jeff looked really scared. . . . I was thinking, "God! What do I do now? Do I take his hand? Do I hug him? Do I talk to him? Do I . . . ?"

When the therapist told Tony, the second sibling in the same family, that he needed a divorce from one of his parents, Tony thought it was from his father.

The therapist disagreed, however, saying that Tony had not been close to his father. Tom described his reactions to these comments:

> I just remember looking at my dad and that just cut so deep . . . that really hurt. . . . And then I was feeling more uncomfortable because I had to take care of his feelings and Mom's feelings and Mike's and now Tony's. Mom was getting upset with that . . . . I guess her bad feelings just multiplied. Cuz she was feeling, "Oh, God, this isn't going to work and this hour isn't going to be a miracle and we're all going to go out of here dancing and . . . . " I could see it building up cuz she was hearing, for like the first time, how everybody felt and the real feelings just made everything worse for her.

When asked to respond to the therapist's statement in the session that he, Mike, and Tony were all very open, Tom responded:

> I was embarrassed. I didn't want to hear it. . . . I mean I don't really . . . . I get embarrassed and I didn't . . . and I don't want to be embarrassed . . . any uncomfortableness. I didn't want any of that, and yet there it was, and it was going to happen over and over again. So I tried to shut it out by playing the game, you know, comfort Mom, comfort Dad, even though normally I would've comforted Mom, but I would've walked away from Dad.

In response to an incident in the session with Jeff, his oldest brother, Tom said:

> Again I lied, I didn't want to get to know Jeff. I had absolutely no interest in him, and that made me feel guilty, so I started to cry. Then I felt more guilty when . . . [the therapist] picked it up as being something real . . . cuz I was so good at playing those games, and I was just the greatest actor . . . as you saw . . . I could just lie. . . . If I had to watch the whole thing over I could pick out everything I did and say, "I didn't mean that, I didn't mean that, and I didn't mean that." I could tell you just what I was thinking because I have played the games so many times that I know the parts by heart. Yeah, I was too open about it. . . . because, okay . . . I was being open about most of it, but I was just in there to play a little game.

Tom's reaction to Jeff's expression of rage during the therapy session was as follows:

I picked up fear from everyone. . . . I was so scared. I had never . . . I expected, you know, never to see that side of Jeff, ever! I was thinking about what he had to do, what he was brought up to do, holding, you know, holding everything inside, and it made me scared. . . . And it made me that way because the way I wanted to be . . . I wanted to be somebody who didn't need anyone, who didn't, you know, have to show anger, who didn't give a damn. And when I saw it in Jeff it scared me. . . . Then he [Jeff] said, "Anger is illogical." All the fear went away, and it just . . . anger just rushed in. I was so mad at him for saying that. . . . For the first time, he was showing some feelings, you know, some anger, even some love . . . and he'd never shown any . . . any feeling at all, except when he was mad he would, you know, go away. And then to see it all . . . except when he said that [anger is illogical], I just blew up inside. I didn't say anything; I just sat back and thought, "Well, time for me not to care anymore." After he'd just gotten me scared and then I cared for him. At that moment I thought, "God, I really love him, and now look what I've done to him!" And I was thinking Mom and Dad didn't have anything to do with it at all. The way he was acting was because, you know, the anger and holding everything in was because of me. And that's what scared me the most, is that I felt so responsible for everything he was feeling . . . because of what I had said and because of how I had acted toward him.

As is typical of fourth children, Tom takes all the blame for the pain in the family and is overly dramatic about it. He feels relief when someone in the family recognizes and admits some of the pain. Jeff's sudden disclaimer of the pain's importance (i.e., by saying his feelings and pain are illogical) can be perceived by Tom as putting the burden back on him, however.

Identity and Sense of Well-Being

Just as the perceptual orientation of fourth children is influenced by the family system, so is the development of their identity. Their sense of well-being is related to their functional roles, the success with which they perform these roles, and the family's acceptance of what they do. Their individual needs to belong to the family and to be accepted as separate, unique, valuable family members interface with their search for identity. Their perception of the world influences their evaluation and interpretation of their place and their contribution to the family.

Self-Esteem and Well-Being

The self-esteem of fourth children is based in part on their ability to put things together and derive goals that contribute to the unity and harmony of the system, whether the system is a family, a relationship, or a small group. Their ability to notice everything that is happening in the system and fit it into the whole is important to them. Similarly, fourth children derive self-esteem from taking over the burdens or tasks that are difficult, painful, or disruptive for individuals or the family system as a whole. Their special place is that they are the supporters. (Their self-esteem is enhanced only if they receive recognition and approval for this role, however.) Consequently, they have a sense of well-being when they have a secure sense that the system is moving toward its purposes and that the system is in harmony.

Because they are system experts, who can read incompleteness in individuals as well as in systems, and because feeling part of a whole enhances their self-esteem, fourth children feel responsible for contributing to somebody else's completeness. Picking up someone's pain and/or confusion, they examine it, make sense of it, draw conclusions about it, and return it in a holistic way. They also reflect cognitively and personally on the emotional state of others. As students of human behavior, they can usually mimic other people very well in a kind of irritative or entertaining way. Because of this, they can teach others about themselves, which makes fourth children feel good and then they look content, excited, and happy.

Fourth children have a secure sense of who they are, because they have no boundary issues. Their awareness of their limitations in trying to maintain unity and harmony in a constantly changing, complex family system diminishes their self-esteem, however. They feel limited because the job is endless, because so many factors can disrupt the family. Therefore, they have a strong need for recognition and approval.

Many fourth children are uneasy if they have too much power, because it makes them too responsible for the system. They prefer that power and responsibility be evenly distributed. When fourth children are asked to perform, however, they perform beautifully. If given the leadership, they check with others, obtain input on decisions, and distribute the power.

Threats to Well-Being

Fourth children feel threatened when families are not achieving their purposes because of a lack of harmony and organization, when the Gestalt is too large, when others give them too much personal responsibility, when they are burdened with pain, and when they feel responsible for what is happening in the system. They also feel threatened when leadership in families or in social groups is autocratic and unfair.

Responses to Threats to Well-Being

When the disruption in the family is overwhelming, fourth children assume that the system is too big. Thus, they restrict the size of the system, cutting people and information out of their perception to lighten the load until they feel safe. They appear to be totally irresponsible at such times; the pain and disarray of the system is too much for them.

Fourth children are naturally impulsive, but their impulsive behavior is sometimes related to psychological threats. In this case, impulsiveness is based in part on the extent to which they absorb the tension and psychological pain of those around them. Because they perceive such tension and pain as a threat to the harmony of the system, fourth children incorporate the source of the danger into themselves. After they have absorbed as much as possible, they need some way to unload. This may result in seemingly impulsive and irrational behavior. Fourth children may also become "cute" and/or "babyish" when tense and anxious.

One of the most frustrating characteristics of fourth children is their refusal to accept responsibility for their behaviors when they act out the family's pain. Because tensions were not really theirs in the first place, and because they took the burdens on themselves only for the good of the system, they feel justified in doing whatever they must to relieve the burden.

When burdens become overwhelming, such as the assignment of too much personal responsibility, fourth children can develop protective layers of helplessness that are very difficult to penetrate. They perceive themselves as helpless and thus do not assert themselves. They tend to terminate their efforts before they discover what they can really accomplish, primarily because it is more comfortable to bring closure at that point. In the extreme form of helplessness, fourth children are paralyzed as a result of too much pain and do nothing.

Siblings' Needs from Others

Like everyone else in the family, fourth children need positive affirmation. Explicit expressions of the impact that fourth children have on the system, particularly the positive impact, build their self-esteem. They need this information because they blame themselves for the pain in the family, and they assume that others blame them also. Although their impulsive actions sometimes cause distress for the family, they need approval and recognition for what they do to counteract their feelings of responsibility for pain in the family.

They also need to be reminded that they are not always the cause of problems in the family or in their relationships.

In dysfunctional families, the parents rarely acknowledge the positive contributions of their children; they focus instead on what is painful, wrong, and hopeless. Fourth children receive the message that they must do something about family pain, but that nothing they do will be effective. Fourth children need information about their contributions to disruptions in the family, but the information should be given in a particular way. When others are explicit in accepting responsibility for their own part in the disruption, fourth children can accept responsibility for their part without assuming responsibility for the whole problem.

If fourth children have all the information they need, they are not symptomatic. Because they prematurely close their view of the whole, fourth children need information from others. The kind and amount of information needed vary from situation to situation. To fourth children, explanations may sound like justifications for making a request so they become stubborn and justify themselves. When the information is linked to overall purpose, however, they see the information as relevant and integrate it into their perceptions. By this process, fourth children can learn to recognize their contribution to system goals. When they notice their outcomes and own them, it improves their confidence.

Tables that summarize the characteristic response patterns for fourth siblings are in the Appendix.

Interaction of Sibling Positions in Marriage, Parenting, and Families

The interactions between sibling positions are inescapably a part of the fabric of marriages and families. The interaction of complementary patterns in marriages creates both harmony and conflict, function and dysfunction. Harmony develops from the familiarity of the patterns. The differences in the patterns provide interest and intrigue in the relationship because of the variation; however, these same differences also serve as fuel for conflict. Furthermore, the sibling interaction patterns apply in relationships in other settings as well, such as work, school, and social activities.

CHAPTER *8*

Sibling Combinations in Marital Dyads

Each spouse brings to the marriage sibling response patterns developed from the unique experiences and sibling assignments in his or her family of origin. These patterns interact with all other patterns and factors in the marriage, weaving diverse marital configurations. Consequently, each marital dyad has both its own unique "personality" and some characteristic patterns traceable to the sibling position characteristics of each spouse.

Each dyad has the potential for both functional and dysfunctional interaction. Specific combinations of sibling positions in marriages are not more functional than others. Sibling combinations in marriage are functional when both spouses are psychologically healthy, have separated from their family of origin, and have a stable self-esteem. In addition, they must have developed constructive strategies for resolving conflict, and they must accept and recognize each other's styles of thinking, feeling, and interacting. Sibling patterns in marriage become dysfunctional when the patterns are exaggerated or shut down, when they persist over time and contexts; when one or both spouses cannot accept the other's style of thinking, feeling, or interacting; or when unresolved issues in the family of origin surface in the marital dynamics. Crises and stress in their extended families that cause the spouses to assume childhood roles become marital issues if the demands of the family of origin interfere with the services, resources, and quality of the relationships within their own family, especially within the marital relationship.

The ways in which the three characteristic response patterns for each sibling position interact within each marital combination may be influenced by such things as family size, spacing of siblings, multiple births, gender differences, stages of development, deaths of siblings or parents, and miscarriages. The exact influence of these factors becomes apparent only when the specifics of each family are examined. The four basic sibling positions interact with gender to form 16 different marital sibling combinations. Within each marital combination, there are many diverse interactional patterns. The patterns described in this chapter are representative rather than exhaustive. Although some of these patterns may be considered dysfunctional for some couples, the same patterns are satisfactory for other couples. For example, regardless of sibling positions, some people live happily with chaos and high stress levels whereas others require order and low stress levels to be happy and satisfied. The best way to determine whether these sibling patterns are dysfunctional and should be modified is to determine the degree of dissatisfaction that couples experience in their marriages and the contribution of sibling patterns to the dissatisfaction.

Siblings Married to Siblings Just Younger or Just Older

In marriages between those who were adjacent siblings in their families of origin functional family roles are complementary. Although their relationship with their spouse is different from that with their siblings, they know a great deal about each other as spouses because of these complementary roles. The "knowing" may be on an intuitive level, but it is there in the form of expectations, issues, and recognition of interaction patterns.

First Siblings Married to Second Siblings

The marriage of first siblings to second siblings generally results in a style of interaction that is argumentative and emotionally emphatic with an abundance of direct comments that openly focus on the personal problems of the partners or on the issues in the marriage relationship. Problem solving for them centers on obtaining a resolution. Both first and second siblings emphasize an informational process that keeps information visible and obvious in their discussions. This makes open and emotionally risky interactions an acceptable reality within their marriage.

This pattern of interaction makes sense in that both first and second siblings are oriented to looking at the parts and interacting with individuals. Thus, when they are in their cognitive patterns, their conversations may consist of logical or intellectually toned exchanges of ideas, facts, thoughts, or interpretations. The tendency to use cognitive statements reflects the basic perceptual preference (logical and rational) of the first sibling and is supported by the

ability of the second sibling to polarize to this intellectual and explicit orientation. The second sibling's polarization to either a highly cognitive or highly
emotional stance in stressful interpersonal encounters, combined with the role
assignment to maintain stability in the system, facilitates the adaptation to the
first sibling's style.

Complementary roles function well in the marital combination of Jeannette,
a first sibling, married to Monty, a second sibling. Jeannette was assigned in
her family of origin to support, make explicit, and enforce family rules, values,
and expectations, particularly those of her parents. Monty's assignment in his
family of origin was to respond to increased maintenance needs in the family
by perceiving and supporting implicit unconscious elements in family rules
and relationships and to reduce the discrepancy between overt and covert rules
and values. Monty was concerned with the quality of the performance on the
job, rather than just finishing the job. Because second siblings often monitor
the quality of the performance in an implicit way, at times Monty seemed to be
focused on results much as Jeannette was focused on them.

Jeannette was accustomed to managing her own environment and was very
productive. At times, she appeared to Monty to be so independent that she did
not need anything from him. On the other hand, Monty seemed to sense her
moods and felt responsible for them. This pattern worked well for them much
of the time, but problems arose occasionally. For example, Jeannette was
sometimes so involved in independently finishing her projects that Monty
perceived her behavior as a personal rejection. He lost the feeling that he had a
unique place in their marriage and questioned his identity and worth. Jeannette would sometimes dismiss her part in the creation of this situation, telling
Monty that he was imagining things, so that it became "his" problem. This
dysfunctional pattern sometimes escalated because Jeannette did not receive
recognition for doing her job, which threatened her self-esteem. Then, in an
effort to convince him that she was doing a good job Jeannette would fight
with Monty about who was right. For this couple, the pattern was temporary
and usually surfaced in a specific context; for other couples, however, it can
become part of all interactions.

Because of their perceptual orientations, Jeannette often focused on explicit
facts and details, and Monty focused on implicit information. Results of their
interactions were both positive and negative, because they did not always
understand each other's frame of reference. On the other hand, Jeannette's
detailed information helped Monty bring implicit information into the
awareness of both, and this additional information enriched the relationship.

When Monty discussed problems in an analytical style with Jeannette, he
encouraged her to focus on her emotional behavior in relation to tension
between them. If she saw the relevance of her emotions, she responded directly
to them. In return, Jeannette helped Monty when he was too focused and

burdened by emotions. She reminded him that she appreciated his loving concern for her, but that he was too responsible for her feelings.

Sometimes, Jeannette ignored or denied her emotions and Monty would try to take care of her by either confronting her about her emotions or accepting them as his own. A fight would erupt after Jeannette's denial of her emotions, followed by depression for one or both of them. The amount and intensity of the emotional load of the second sibling interacting with the degree of threat experienced by the first sibling regulate the size of the conflict and stress for the couple.

First siblings thrive in a marriage when their spouse confirms that they perform their tasks very well and that they behave appropriately in social situations. Second sibling spouses may recognize the importance and centrality of their first sibling spouse, but problems may arise in the relationship if they do not make this knowledge and their appreciation explicit. The implicit messages of appreciation that second sibling spouses believe have been sent are often not received by the first sibling spouse. Consequently, conflict can build around these issues without either understanding the source.

Second siblings thrive in a marriage with a first sibling spouse who constantly affirms their importance in the marriage. The affirmation must be both implicitly and explicitly congruent. This gives the second sibling spouses a feeling of a unique place without the clamor of underlying double messages and emotional debris.

Multigenerational issues for this marital combination are almost always nested in the relationships that the spouses have with their mothers and fathers. Each can be overly responsible for his or her parents, making the other feel neglected. First children are responsible for father and for every member of the family to father. Thus, a first son who continues to take care of his mother after his marriage is actually feeling a responsibility to his father, not his mother. Without this clarification, he may fight continually with his mother and with his spouse without resolution. Similarly, first siblings of either sex may carry unresolved issues of their father in the form of depression, irresponsibility, and headaches.

Second siblings may be so connected to the unresolved issues and emotional debris in their family of origin that they cannot be out of contact with them without exhibiting great anxiety. Conversely, they may polarize and be highly disengaged and cognitive about their extended family's problems. If the issues are not resolved for second siblings, the same issues and the pattern of disengagement and cognitive analysis may surface in their marriage.

Second Siblings Married to Third Siblings

Third siblings are responsible for the balance in relationships. They are relationship experts. All third siblings go in and out of relationships, however, regardless of the quality of the relationships. Thus, it may appear to their second sibling spouse that they are ignoring the feelings and needs of their spouse. In spite of this apparent neglect, third siblings feel deeply and can identify feelings if they perceive them as a legitimate part of the context. Consequently, if the conditions are right, third and second siblings can share feelings and negotiate conflict in their marriages in a productive way.

Bob, a third sibling, often identified issues and made explicit connections to what was happening in his relationship with his wife, Lou. This was helpful to Lou, a second sibling, who could more easily read the implicit structure and messages in their marital system. It was also reassuring for Lou to know that Bob was really committed to their marriage, because it meant that she rarely questioned her place in their relationship. Like most thirds, Bob needed to put distance between himself and his relationship with Lou in order to remain balanced and neutral. Although Lou was sometimes confused by Bob's behavior, she was not threatened by it because she knew he was committed to her. Because Lou did not personalize his behavior, Bob did not become defensive when she asked him about it. This gave him a choice of possible responses, thus facilitating a happier marriage.

Some third siblings are not firmly committed to their marriage and give many conflicting implicit and explicit messages. This constantly erodes the identity and well-being of the second sibling spouse, who then has no secure place and may respond with helpless, dependent behavior. Often third siblings interpret the demand in the relationship from this kind of behavior as a limit to their choices, and they respond by in-and-out behavior.

The going away behavior can be frustrating to a second sibling spouse because third sibling spouses turn inward to process and resolve relationship problems. In a time of conflict, third siblings often withdraw, physically and/or emotionally, process the experience, and return to report a resolution. The second sibling feels left out of the process, is caught with unresolved emotions, and has no understanding of the way in which the third sibling spouse arrived at a resolution.

Several things can happen in this situation. Although third siblings do not usually perceive a need to be specific about their internal processing, they are always very aware of connections and disconnections. Detecting that they have disconnected from their spouse in some way, they attempt to reconnect. If the second sibling spouse can then be specific about what is needed, third siblings are willing to supply missing information and connect it to other pieces. The second sibling spouse may respond positively and helpfully, and the conflict can be resolved.

If the third sibling spouse does not attempt to reconnect, the second sibling spouse does not have sufficient data to understand the way in which the third sibling reached a given resolution about the relationship issue. Without this information, second sibling spouses may make assumptions based on their feelings, a reading of the underlying structure, and past marital interactions. Third siblings may never know that for a time they were disconnected from their spouse, as second siblings then act on these assumptions as if they were absolutely accurate. This procedure can be disastrous if the assumptions are wrong, rewarding if they are right.

When neither Bob nor Lou was threatened, the lack of clarity about a relationship issue or the resolution of a problem often generated a speculative and analytical questioning approach. This led the spouses to examine a number of solutions, to clear the air, and to resolve the problem together. To an observer, their interaction might appear to be without affective tones because they tended to respond in a noncommittal or ambivalent manner. Sometimes each kept the interactional focus on the statements of the other through brief intermediary comments that continued the other's flow of statements. This provided a tentative and emotionally safe tone to many of their interchanges.

Although third siblings are experts on the issues and dynamics in relationships, they are often unwilling to take a stand in marital exchanges for fear of disrupting the relationship balance. As a result, third siblings seem to prefer a more tentative and often emotionally ambivalent (in-and-out) style in interpersonal communication that may curb the open and direct dialogue of marital issues between partners. This neutral approach to issue resolution fits the role assignment of third siblings to ensure a balance between relationship separateness and connectedness. It is a way of keeping their choices open.

A strength that Lou brought to her marriage to Bob was her ability to sense his emotions and needs, and to respond to those needs without an explicit request. When second siblings assist by making the implicit messages explicit, the job of regulating and balancing the relationship is easier for third siblings. Because Bob's focus was on issues, he sometimes prematurely limited the context of a marital issue and ignored important details and feelings. He would be so focused on what he perceived as the issue that he offended Lou by ignoring her wishes and feelings. Lou was confused, because she did not understand what was happening and thought that nothing she said or did was considered. Lou emphasized the importance of their feelings in understanding the situation.

Unless second sibling spouses polarize cognitively in this situation, their third sibling spouse's pattern of limiting the context can create conflict for the marital relationship. If they polarize or integrate the cognitive and the affective components within a given context, the style of second siblings complements the cognitive style of third sibling spouses and adds important pieces to the interaction. To the outsider this kind of marital interaction seems to be a socially appropriate, superficial, tentative, and emotionally safe approach to resolving marital issues.

One reason that Bob failed to note details and to make them part of the context was that he was busy rearranging and synthesizing existing ideas and data into new ideas. It was very disconcerting to Lou that Bob did not seek information and meaning from her, because she was often focused more on people and process than content. When third siblings ignore or dismiss the underlying structure and the implicit messages that second siblings perceive as important, second siblings feel ignored and dismissed also, or at least not validated as important in the relationship. At the same time, third siblings can be thoroughly confused by their second sibling spouse's inability to see the relevance of connections, and they feel unimportant.

As confusion, frustration, and other feelings intensify in this situation, second siblings absorb their spouse's feelings and tensions as if these feelings and tensions were their own, usually at an implicit level. With their third sibling spouse focused on issues, second siblings often find it difficult to identify, label, and sort out their own feelings; they become blocked and burdened with details and emotions. As a result, it is difficult for second siblings to find a structure that makes sense. When third sibling spouses decide to help by supplying what they consider new information or by urging their second sibling spouse to focus on the "real" issues, the second sibling may ignore the additional data and appear stubborn. The conflict accelerates, because neither partner feels understood. Each goes into defensive posturing and maneuvering.

On the other hand, third siblings recognize many relationship aspects on an intuitive level. They may sense that their second sibling spouse needs to process feelings, and if they do not feel threatened psychologically, they can be sufficiently detached to allow their spouse to sort through the emotional debris in a beneficial way. Second siblings contribute to this interaction pattern by processing implicit and explicit data at an implicit level and acting on the information as if everyone processes it in the same way and has the same knowledge, when, in fact, they do not.

When Lou and Bob were psychologically threatened at the same time, they found it very difficult to communicate or to feel important to each other. Lou lost her sense of having a unique and separate place in the marriage and had very little energy to cope with Bob. When threatened, Bob found it hard to focus on feelings. Lou tended to absorb his feelings as her own, resulting in unclear boundaries and a confused sense of identity. Lou's need for him to admit his own feelings was frustrating and confusing to Bob, as he was focused on the issues in the situation. This need became a burden to him, as he sensed that his choices were limited in some very powerful ways.

When they are threatened, second siblings can be very stubborn and appear uncooperative and rebellious. They may become highly emotional or highly intellectual, detached or overly involved. Because third siblings do not feel appreciated in this context, they may appear apathetic or inappropriately carefree. If their spouse is seeking some kind of action from them, such as a decision, third siblings appear ambivalent and do not commit to a choice. In the presence of discrepant ideas or feelings or interpersonal conflict with their spouse, they may reject all moves toward them and distort ideas and processes proffered by their spouse. Sometimes, they deal with pain, confusion, and pressure by withdrawing. This can become a dysfunctional pattern.

Second siblings thrive in a marriage with a third sibling if their spouse recognizes and is explicit about the contributions they make to the marriages. Their need to have an identity separate from that of their spouse and others with well-defined boundaries is supported by a healthy third sibling spouse. Third siblings thrive in a marriage with a second sibling if they are appreciated by their spouse for their ability to discover appropriate and meaningful rules of relationships and apply them in the marriage.

The multigenerational issues in this sibling combination marriage may appear very similar for both spouses, but there are some distinctions. For example, both second and third siblings may have unresolved issues in the family of origin that keep them overly involved with their mothers. Second siblings may have been unable to separate clearly from their mother's emotions and needs. They may also be involved with their father if they are fighting their mother's issues with him. Third siblings' involvements with their mother may be a means of keeping her involved in her own marriage. In other words, they may be convinced that their mother is likely to leave the parents' marriage. As long as third siblings repeat the patterns that kept her in the marriage in the past, there is hope that their mother will stay in the marriage. They may be involved with father in the same way for the same reason.

Third Siblings Married to Fourth Siblings

A third sibling and fourth sibling who are married have little conflict about their roles in the marriage, and they usually work very well together in their respective assignments. Both are invested in harmony and balance. Because third siblings were responsible for the dynamics and quality of their parents' marital relationship, it is easy for them to focus on the quality of their own marital relationship and the balance in all other family dyadic relationships, including those in their extended family. Although third siblings know a great deal about their own marital relationship, they have blind spots and biases. Fourth siblings complement their third sibling spouse's focus on dyadic relationships by being responsible for family unity and harmony so that the family can be purposeful in meeting its goals.

In marital relationships, third siblings' identity and sense of well-being are associated with the stability of their marital relationship. Fourth siblings' self-esteem and sense of well-being are fostered by a clear sense of purpose in their marriage, maintenance of marital harmony, and a knowledge that they make a positive difference in the marital system. They need constant approval and encouragement from their spouse to continue to make the kinds of contributions at which they excel.

Because the manner in which third and fourth siblings connect to family members is complementary, Ed, a third sibling, and Karen, a fourth sibling, found it easy to feel connected to each other. Ed connected to all dyadic relationships by discovering and enforcing rules about the degree and nature of relationship dynamics, such as closeness, conflict, dependency, intrusiveness, and loyalty. In order to determine what is going on in the family, Karen connected to each family member by being loving, by caring, and by locating and repairing any disruptions in the system. Karen had immediate, almost impulsive, reactions and was highly demonstrative in her expressions of feelings and ideas. She openly expressed warmth and closeness, by both actions and words. Spontaneous hugs and "I love you" messages were not unusual throughout day-to-day activities with Ed. He loved this demonstrativeness, as it promoted an ongoing, explicit connection with his spouse. At times, Ed was also warm and explicit about his own feelings.

Although Ed wanted to remain connected, he did not want to be intrusive. Therefore, he appeared disconnected at times, even in his committed relationship with Karen. His in-and-out behavior was sometimes confusing to Karen, because it at times had nothing to do with their current marital interaction. No matter whether the tension is part of a relationship issue or whether the third sibling spouse has brought it from other contexts, fourth siblings tend to take on tensions and stress from their spouse. Consequently, when Ed moved out of the relationship to resolve the tension, Karen urged him to stay and work it out. In her family of origin, Karen learned to act out the tensions in the family by fighting with her third sibling to focus parents and other family members on the problems. Both Ed and Karen brought such fight patterns into the marriage.

As in all functional marital combinations that include third siblings, the in-and-out behavior of third siblings is not a problem as long as the spouse understands it and/or is secure in the marital relationship. Sometimes Karen interpreted Ed's in-and-out behavior to mean that he blamed her for the pain and disruption in the harmony in their marital relationship. In response, she appeared totally irresponsible and helpless and engaged in random, distracting behavior that did not contribute to resolution. Clearly, those in this marital sibling combination may find it difficult to solve problems if they are both threatened at the same time.

Although Ed felt secure in their marital relationship, he seldom thought to use the relationship for support and tended to work out problems alone. That pattern changed, however, if Karen made an explicit offer of support; it was natural for Karen to support Ed in this way. Fourth siblings are loyal in working to meet their spouse's goals if they were included in the decision-making process. Conversely, when fourth siblings receive little or no information about the process of the decision, their spouse appears autocratic to them, and their inclination is to sabotage these decisions usually in a very obvious way. This is very confusing to the third sibling spouse, who may think that the decision is serving the relationship.

On the other hand, if fourth siblings have a decision to make, they attempt to involve their third sibling spouse in the process. If it is clear that the effects of the decision are relevant to the relationship, the spouse may participate. If there is no apparent relevance, the spouse may advise the fourth sibling to make the decision alone. Confusion may arise from the fact that fourth siblings are not necessarily seeking help in making the decision, but involvement and investment from their spouse. When told to make their own decisions, they sometimes are hurt and angry. In the resulting conflict, the third sibling fights not to lose choices, and the fourth sibling tries to determine who is to blame for the disruption in the relationship.

In their family of origin, fourth siblings are sometimes so focused on the family goal of unity and harmony that they do not perceive relationships as worthwhile in themselves. Thus, they may subtly discount their marital relationship. When this happens, third sibling spouses may feel disconnected and unappreciated. They may go away to deal with their pain and try to resolve the problem. In response to the distance and disruption they feel, fourth siblings immediately assume the blame and try to make it right in some way. For example, they may plan a favorite dinner or be unusually attentive. Because most of this interacting pattern is on the implicit level, third siblings find it unconnected to anything of importance and withdraw further to make sense of what is happening. Unless interrupted in a constructive way, this pattern can escalate into a dysfunctional and common pattern in the marriage.

Third and fourth siblings make sense of their world in complementary ways, but they have similar problems in what they overlook. Third siblings examine connections, correlations, and issues in a given context, while fourth siblings think in terms of total systems, conclusions, and outcomes. Consequently, they may summarize experiences superficially, prematurely, and dramatically. The absence of important details in their perceptions can cause confusion, misunderstanding, and tentative decisions. If neither spouse is threatened, they manage with what they have or discover the details through what each knows.

Fourth siblings need their spouse to remind them that they are not wholly responsible for problems in their relationship and not to blame for all tensions and feelings that their spouse carries. They need help in accepting responsibility for only their parts in conflictual or emotional situations. The more that their spouse admits to his or her contribution (whether action, ideas, or feeling), the more fourth siblings have a sense of well-being. They need explicit verbalizations that they make a positive difference in the marriage, because they thrive on approval.

Third siblings thrive in a marriage with a fourth sibling when their spouse gives them constant messages of appreciation and does not limit their freedom by making choices for them. They want help from their spouse in creating legitimate choices. However, when they feel threatened, they need their spouse to remind them that they are not alone, that they are loved and appreciated, and that moving away from the context makes it impossible for their spouse to help them make decisions. At the same time, they need permission and acceptance to be in and out of the context.

Third siblings usually remain invested in the quality of their parents' marriage and other relationships in their family of origin, often including the marriages of each of their siblings. Sometimes, they assume a similar interest and investment in the marriages of the parents and siblings of their spouse. The more they discover and understand the rules of all these marital relationships and apply them, the greater their sense of well-being.

Fourth siblings remain connected to their family of origin, whether through letters, personal visits, or telephone calls. Third sibling spouses seem to understand this connection, and it is not a problem unless either or both of their families of origin are dysfunctional. Then third and fourth sibling spouses may fight about resources, such as time and money, that are siphoned from the marital relationship, eroding mutual goals and companionship.

Other Sibling Marital Combinations

Although the patterns of marital combinations that involve nonadjacent siblings are complementary, the gaps between siblings contribute to different marital issues and form their own patterns of harmony and conflict.

First Siblings Married to Third Siblings

The functional family role assignments of first and third siblings bring a productive pattern to their marriage. First siblings support and sponsor explicit family rules, values, and expectations. Both first and third siblings are invested in the marital relationship rules. Third siblings need to know the rules so that they can use them to balance relationships. Both of these sibling roles serve the productivity needs of the family, because they facilitate the completion of tasks and family interactions. Values are enforced and expectations met through explicitness and agreement about the rules.

Although first and third siblings may be in agreement about some implicit rules in the marriage, implicit rules can become a source of conflict if, for example, one spouse makes a rule explicit by changing it in a dispute. Annette, a first sibling, tended to be bossy and independent, while Clyde, a third sibling, negotiated to establish his freedom if he felt the need. An implicit rule that developed easily in their marriage was based on Annette's assumption that she would make most of the decisions, efficiently and correctly. She assumed that Clyde agreed, because he did not disagree. Clyde, however, thought that it was appropriate for Annette to make decisions only if her decision did not reduce his freedom.

The combination of the two assumptions worked very well as an implicit rule when Clyde agreed with the decision, when he was ambivalent about it, or when the decision seemed irrelevant to his activities. Because many decisions fell into one of these three categories, Annette thought all was well. Any time that Annette made a decision that Clyde perceived as a limit to his freedom, however, they had a fight about it. Annette was surprised, confused, and threatened by the conflict, because the patterns of decision making usually worked for them.

Annette tried to obtain detailed information about every part of what she perceived as a criticism of her performance. Clyde tried to discuss the issues, and they both became confused. For Annette, the fight was about a rule change; for Clyde it was about a rule clarification. Because Clyde was a good negotiator and usually looked at all sides of a conflict, he eventually gave Annette the information she needed. Gradually, they learned what the pattern meant to each of them; Annette learned to ask if the decision was one she should make, and Clyde learned to identify his issues clearly for himself and for Annette when decisions had to be made.

Unless they are psychologically threatened, third siblings can and do supply all the information they have to answer their spouse's questions. They also indicate connections providing their first sibling spouse with a different way of looking at the situation. Because of their focus elsewhere, neither first nor third siblings may express their feelings in this situation; however, both can identify and label their feelings and make them part of the information in the conflict if they are aware of their relevance.

First siblings are threatened when they are confused; they compartmentalize information because they lose a sense of the whole. If third siblings feel threatened and if they sense that their spouse is not listening or integrating new information to move toward some kind of compromise, they disengage by moving away, physically or psychologically. This is disconcerting and confusing to the first sibling spouse, as it shuts off the supply of information.

When threatened psychologically, Annette felt that she had failed in some way and believed her situation to be hopeless. When she generalized this to her marital relationship, Clyde perceived her as "stony and thunderous in countenance, immovable, and unfeeling." In conversations, no matter how mundane the topic, she was dogmatic, insisted that she was right, and distanced herself from Clyde. She often dismissed what he said as irrelevant.

When Clyde was threatened by Annette's behavior or feelings of personal failure, he exaggerated his own patterns in response to her. The more confused and distant Annette behaved, the more confined and trapped Clyde felt. With no movement toward resolution, it seemed to him that his choices were being eliminated. He responded by adopting an uncaring and ambivalent attitude and eventually would not talk with Annette. He appeared to turn off all feelings as a way of protection and disappeared into his own world. It was easy for him to reject or distort Annette's ideas and feelings, because he felt inundated and chaotic.

These are extreme patterns that may occur when both first and third spouses are psychologically threatened at the same time. The interaction spirals into one loop of dysfunction after another. This marriage was not basically dysfunctional, however. Through the years, Clyde and Annette developed strategies for supporting each other. They learned to understand what was happening to them and to discuss it.

After marriage, many first siblings remain connected to their family of origin much as they were connected when they were growing up. Some of the alliances developed in childhood carry forward into their adult lives. For example, if younger siblings came to them for advice or resources as children, they may continue to do so as adults. If there is no drain on the resources of the marital relationship, third sibling spouses understand these family interactions, viewing them as a way of staying connected. Their own needs to remain connected to their parents and to other relationships in their families are likewise understood by their first sibling spouses.

First Siblings Married to Fourth Siblings

The combination of first siblings married to fourth siblings brings together the oldest and the youngest of the four basic sibling positions. First siblings view all sibling roles from the top. Perhaps perceiving their younger siblings as spoiled or demanding, they have little explicit knowledge of the way in which fourth siblings view the world and what they do in their family job assignments. On the other hand, fourth siblings view sibling job assignments from the bottom. Whereas first siblings may be missing information about younger siblings, fourth siblings may have much more information about first siblings;

some of it may be distorted, however. Fourth siblings may see first siblings as distant, parental figures who served them in some way or who played with them and took them places. Much of this information is on an implicit level.

The responsibility of first siblings for individuals in the family dovetails nicely with the responsibility of fourth siblings for the whole family system. Their sense of interpersonal responsibility and their social interaction patterns can be a complementary force or a source of conflict in the marriage. First siblings are more content with one-on-one interactions, observing more and interacting less with a group of people. Fourth siblings, on the other hand, are equally comfortable with individuals or groups. The pattern is complementary when the marital combination of a first and fourth sibling interacts with a group if both spouses are content with their roles. The fourth sibling spouse smooths the way for the first sibling spouse by socializing with the group as a whole. This leaves the first sibling free to interact with one individual at a time or to be an observer as the group interacts. These patterns occur in both family and social groups.

Pete, a fourth sibling, was a very good host. People sensed that he cared for them as he made sure that everyone was comfortable. He felt responsible for tension and disruption, so he mixed easily with everyone, teasing this one, smoothing over any disagreement, and maintaining high energy. Because this was antithetical to her style of interacting, Tamara, a first sibling, was content to let Pete "run the show." She usually focused her attention on one person at a time or moved from one small group to another. Their friends liked to go to their home and enjoyed their parties.

The self-esteem of first siblings is correlated to the approval of others, particularly authority figures and those in meaningful relationships with the first siblings. They believe that they are experts in socially appropriate behavior, because their parents gave them a great deal of instruction so that they could represent the expectations and values of the family. Fourth siblings are social experts, too. Although there is no explicit pressure from parents to be experts, they learn social skills from their job assignment of maintaining peace and keeping the family working together. For some first and fourth sibling spouses, implicit messages of "rightness" in social behavior can be an ongoing implicit issue.

If their fourth sibling spouse criticizes their social behavior, first siblings feel threatened. They may disengage from their spouse by placing the information given by their spouse in a compartment labeled irrelevant and inaccurate; thus, they can rationalize their own behavior as accurate. Disengaging from their spouse makes it unnecessary for them to argue that they are right, even though the separateness may be painful for them. They tend to ignore the pain also, becoming busy or depressed.

Fourth siblings interpret such a disengagement as a disruption in the relationship. They immediately assume the blame for the situation and absorb their spouse's pain, as well as their own. If there is too much pain, fourth siblings act it out to get movement in the relationship and focus the attention of their spouse on the disruption in the system. This may take the form of annoying their spouse, acting in dependent, helpless ways; or going to bed with a terrible headache.

In disruptive situations, the patterns that usually sustain and strengthen a functional marriage eventually surface and assist these couples in working through the conflict. For example, the perceptual patterns of first and fourth siblings bring together most of the information they need to make sense of an incident. If they begin to listen to each other, the additional information provided allows each to understand the other's point of view. Compromise and negotiation become possible. If the marriage is dysfunctional, the incidents accumulate until the couple needs outside help to sort through and resolve the conflict.

Pete and Tamara needed specific things from each other in day-to-day living. Tamara wanted the central place in their relationship. She wanted Pete to give her a great deal of information, not only about herself and her efforts to do things well, but also about himself. Although Pete tended to omit details, he good-naturedly supplied them for Tamara when she asked. On the other hand, Tamara sometimes overwhelmed Pete with the details of her day and her projects. Thus they developed a functional pattern of signals so that each would receive the right amount of information.

Tamara and Pete each needed many messages of recognition and approval, although for different reasons. Pete needed to feel that he made a difference in the marital relationship, and he wanted explicit information about the ways in which he did this. With her ability to notice details and to be explicit, Tamara met this need easily, once she knew what he wanted. Tamara needed approval for the jobs she did and for being "on target" with her projects. Pete's spontaneity and natural appreciation for anything that contributed to a positive climate in their relationship and in their family fit right into Tamara's needs.

First siblings sometimes seem distant to their fourth sibling spouse because they are often involved with personal and family projects that remove them from the marital relationship. Their spouse's demands that they pay more attention to "the family" confuse first siblings, who see themselves as very involved in doing what they perceive must be done for the family. If the marriage is dysfunctional, this pattern can become chronic and generalize into many areas. If the marriage is functional, the pattern may be a source of discomfort for each spouse, but they accept it and work around or through it.

In either case, the situation threatens first siblings because they receive the message that their performance is inadequate.

Issues that involve the extended families sometimes cause difficulty in this sibling marital combination. For example, fourth siblings usually love to attend extended family events, because they can check on everyone and learn what is happening in the family. When their siblings all have families, it is difficult to contact each one to keep up-to-date on events. First siblings understand the need to make contacts, but they may not enjoy all the family gatherings.

Second Siblings Married to Fourth Siblings

Second and fourth siblings both try to maintain a certain atmosphere in the family. Second siblings open clogged channels of communication and reduce the discrepancy between overt and covert rules and values that is sometimes incapacitating to their fourth sibling spouses. Second siblings may panic and behave in chaotic and disruptive ways that may not make sense to their spouse, but moves their spouse toward an expression of personal experience. Fourth siblings try to relieve tension in the system and focus the family on a common cause. This focus helps their second sibling spouse to read more of the underlying structure of the situation. Thus second and fourth siblings force each other to acknowledge what they are thinking and feeling, but not expressing. This keeps each spouse in their family role and relieves each spouse of emotional burdens.

Dan, a second sibling (responsible for individual family members), and Sarah, a fourth sibling (responsible for connections to family members), seemed to work well together in their marriage. Dan's focus on the quality of performance and his absorption of some of the emotional stress in the family facilitated a more peaceful family atmosphere and assisted Sarah in maintaining harmony and unity in the family system. Sarah took on the tensions and stress of individuals to relieve the tension in the family. Because she could identify these emotions, she helped Dan identify and separate his feelings from hers and the children's. This process relieved Dan of excessive emotional baggage.

When things were going well in the family, Sarah was pleasant. When there was a conflict, however she became superficial and behaved as though the marriage was a burden. She felt responsible for all that occurred in their marital and family relationships and collected all the pain associated with the unresolved feelings and issues in the system.

As second and fourth siblings, Dan and Sarah could be tender, sensitive, and caring in their interactions with each other. Dan acted directly on intuitions and feelings, complementing Sarah's immediate, almost impulsive, reactions to people and events. Sarah expressed her feelings and ideas warmly and openly with hugs, kisses, and playfulness, bringing out the same kind of behavior in her husband. Dan could suddenly become rational, distant, and goal-oriented, however. This change in behavior was confusing to Sarah, unless she understood the pattern at either the implicit or explicit level.

In a healthy marriage, second siblings have a clear identity with well-defined boundaries that keep them separate from the identities of their spouse and others. Sarah not only acknowledged Dan's right to have boundaries, but also indicated her own boundaries, thus further legitimizing his boundaries. Their marriage was also strengthened by Dan's knowledge that he was prized in the marriage. By recognizing and explicitly valuing Sarah's warmth, spontaneity, and playfulness, Dan made it clear to Sarah that she made a positive difference in their relationship.

By verifying Dan's boundaries and helping him identify his own feelings, Sarah understood her contributions to conflictual or emotional situations; she did not have to assume responsibility for the whole problem. The more Dan admitted his contributions to marital interaction—whether actions, ideas, or feelings—the more that Sarah developed a strong identity and a sense of self-worth. This was a reciprocal exchange. Each received in specific ways a great deal of approval for his or her activities and identity.

Perceptually, Dan and Sarah also complemented each other. Dan's focus on affect, implicit messages, and process often gave Sarah additional information that she overlooked. He often missed the middle ground between them because he perceived issues in terms of polarities when she was focused on the whole field rather than the parts. Sarah usually had some of this information for him.

Whether their marriage is functional or dysfunctional, second siblings absorb their spouse's feelings and tensions. When Dan felt threatened, it was difficult for him to identify, label, and sort out his own feelings from Sarah's feelings. The more functional the relationship and the less second siblings feel threatened, the more quickly they can separate their feelings from their spouse's feelings and the more their spouse can contribute to the separating process. If not threatened themselves, fourth siblings help second siblings separate by explicitly talking about their own emotions.

Fourth siblings are usually in touch with feelings, both theirs and others, and are rarely confused about whose feelings they are. They are accepted as part of the Gestalt. When fourth siblings are threatened, however, they often misinterpret their spouse's feelings by exaggerating them and by assuming that they, the fourth siblings, have done something to create their spouse's feelings. When Sarah was psychologically threatened, she overdramatized outcomes and conclusions. She would think immediately of the worst possible thing that could happen in the relationship. Usually, she would accuse Dan of rejecting her, or she would focus on their failure as a couple. These behaviors are not helpful to a second sibling spouse who has melded and claimed every feeling in the relationship.

When Dan and Sarah were psychologically threatened at the same time, they bogged down in a sea of emotional debris. With their well-being threatened, second and fourth siblings appear somewhat similar; they seem totally irresponsible and act helpless as they engage in activities that have no clear connection to the situation and do nothing to resolve it. When second and fourth sibling couples get into this cycle, it is impossible for second siblings to find a structure that makes sense to them, because so many incongruent messages are sent. At the same time, the second siblings are mired in excessive and dominant feelings. Fourth siblings are hopelessly lost, because they see only the size and unmanageability of the whole. Until second siblings begin to look at the parts of the situation, fourth siblings cannot move; until fourth siblings begin to recognize the burden of feelings carried by their second sibling spouses, second siblings cannot move.

If second siblings remain connected to their family of origin, they tend to visit each sibling and his or her family separately. Usually, they attend to their mother's needs and by so doing, care for their father as well. Fourth siblings, on the other hand, like family gatherings and may sponsor them. Usually their second sibling spouse is content and sociable at such family gatherings and assists the fourth sibling spouse in positive ways.

Siblings Married to Those in Like Sibling Positions

The combination of siblings married to those in like sibling positions has both potential strengths and potential weaknesses as a result of the similarity in characteristic response patterns. When threatened, these spouses may set up elaborate defense systems that keep them from resolving differences. On the other hand, similar styles of interaction and perceptual patterns can contribute to a very strong foundation for marriage.

First Siblings Married to First Siblings

Two first siblings married to each other may find it very helpful to have the same system role assignments. The marriage runs smoothly when the rules of the relationship are explicit; when they are not explicit, both spouses push for clarity. Because both have the same need to produce explicit results, they are rarely misunderstood when they pursue projects; instead, they lovingly accept each other. These couples can be very happy, productive, and efficient.

Husbands and wives may assume different marital and parental roles in the family, but they perform these roles according to their perception of their assignment. Usually, that perception is governed by their experiences and tutoring in their same sibling positions in their families of origin. Therefore, husbands and wives who are both first siblings expect that the values attached to their roles are known and respected by their spouse and that the rules within the context of their assignments will also be followed by their spouse.

Doug and Marie, both first children, are happy in their marriage when they see themselves as productive individuals and as a successful couple. Each frequently expresses approval of what the other does, contributing to the perceived quality of the marriage. In addition, strategies for sharing resources, time, and talent so that each partner can accomplish his or her goals are an integral part of the marriage.

With their emphasis on responsibility for outcome and productivity Doug and Marie sometimes found themselves in power struggles and symmetrical exchanges. First siblings need to be right, but obviously Doug and Marie could not both be right when there was a difference of opinion. Their arguments escalated as each tried to convince the other that his or her position was the correct one. Moreover, their arguments spread into other areas of their life, often at implicit levels. Finally, they learned to listen and gave each other information until they reached a mutual agreement.

The cognitive styles in the marital combination of first siblings married to first siblings may emphasize facts, details, logic, and analytical processes. Therefore, the marital relationship often lacks an awareness of implicit information and processes. As a result, feelings and personal issues are ignored unless they are clearly relevant. If the two spouses are not psychologically threatened, however, their inclination to process explicitly and to seek additional information brings out much that has been implicit. If either or both are threatened, stressed, or hurried, they tend to discount the implicit and act on incomplete explicit data. Frustration, misunderstanding, and conflict may be the result.

When one spouse is able to express his or her feelings and relate them to what is happening in the interaction, the focus on feelings becomes explicit; this causes the other spouse to examine and express his or her feelings as well. In this marital combination, the expression of feelings can become a source of conflict if one or both partners see the emotion as part of an identity issue. One partner may interpret the other partner's expression of anger or sadness as disapproval, for example.

One spouse may think that feelings are important in a given context, while the other thinks that they are irrelevant and irrational. These differences may be implicit or explicit, but either way, the couple may develop a power struggle over them.

If first sibling spouses are psychologically threatened at the same time, they often adopt a "this is hopeless, we will never be able to work it out" attitude. The degree of depression, stress, and anxiety that accompanies this situation is governed by the degree of dysfunction in each spouse and in the interaction. At this point, each spouse has lost the sense of being on target, of being productive, of being central, and of being important to the other spouse and to the family. When only one spouse is threatened psychologically and the other is explicitly aware of the threat, the nonthreatened spouse can be supportive and encouraging, giving additional and appropriate information.

First siblings married to other first siblings sometimes disagree about the amount of time and resources that should be invested in their extended families. On the other hand, responsible first siblings often reap the rewards of positive and loving relationships with the extended family of their spouse, as well as with their parents and siblings.

Second Siblings Married to Second Siblings

The primary assignment of second siblings to be perceptive and supportive of the unconscious and implicit elements in family rules and relationships greatly influences the marital combination of second siblings married to second siblings. Hannah and Irvin, two second siblings, not only experienced love and affection in their marriage, but also were quite productive in their marriage and in their jobs. They were good at reading the emotional needs and wishes of each other, and each often responded quickly and appropriately to the other without explicit communications. Because both partners read the implicit structure and neither was very competent in making that structure explicit, they sometimes bogged down in the implicit, however. They could move into days of conflict, each acting on different assumptions, before one of them made an explicit statement that enabled them to process the issue.

The fact that second children perceive their world in polarities can strengthen the marriage of two second siblings at times, but it can also add to temporary or chronic dysfunction. When Hannah and Irvin were both polarized in the affective mode, the expression and implicit reading of feelings predominated, and they were not productive. When they were both polarized on task, they functioned much like two first siblings, very rationally and productively.

When two second sibling spouses polarize into the affective mode for long periods of time, dysfunctional patterns may develop. Usually, the spouses meld with each other, mixing and confusing their "debris bags." Their boundaries are often obscured, and they feel lost. In this situation, they no longer have a sense of belonging and of being important to their spouses. This adds to the confusion and leads to further polarization. Sometimes one spouse melds with another person outside the marriage and brings that person's emotions into the marriage.

At times, Irvin and Hannah were quite content to be affective, because it allowed implicit information that helped in the processing of feelings to surface. When one spouse shifted to the cognitive pole, information from two extremes became available so that they could make the implicit explicit, clarifying parts of the structure. They seemed to understand these shifts in polarities intuitively and were generally supportive of each other when they were at opposite ends of the poles. In some contexts, however, the differences in points of view and the amount of affect contributed to conflict and blocked support and understanding.

Second siblings may view productivity as sorting out emotional debris and fulfilling the emotional needs and wishes of their spouse, children, and others with whom they are in contact. When this processing mode is the main emphasis, however, there may be a lack of concrete products to meet the family needs for economic security and daily sustenance. Chaos reigns when both spouses ignore the need for concrete productivity. Even though they both work very hard to find a solution, they become more confused and emotional. If one spouse consistently focuses on the family's emotional needs and the other must assume responsibility for economic security and daily sustenance needs, conflict develops within the relationship; the spouses are operating at opposite poles, and much of the information is implicit. An inability to make the problem explicit intensifies the couple's emotions and sidetracks them from the source of the conflict. These kinds of patterns may arise only occasionally in a marriage, or they may become chronic.

In a dysfunctional marriage, one or both spouses exhibit dependency, helplessness, blurred boundaries, and identity problems. When two second sibling spouses are helpless at the same time, they exaggerate and condone each other's helplessness. In their families of origin, their first sibling often rescued them by clarifying and making explicit the undercurrents or by relieving them of the emotional burdens that they had accumulated. An implicit contract in the marriage may be that one spouse will rescue the other when he or she appears to be helpless.

When there is pain in the marital relationship of two second siblings, they respond in one of two ways. They may run away from it, or they may meld with the pain to the extent that they are unable to move away from it. When one spouse is mired in the pain and the other one runs away from it, the marriage usually needs outside help to identify the issues and assist the spouses in separating from the pain.

Multigenerational issues surface when one or both of the second sibling spouses have not learned to protect their boundaries and to maintain an identity separate from those of extended family members, particularly that of the mother. The need for someone to read and make explicit the implicit currents in their family of origin does not disappear when second siblings marry and set up their own households. The second siblings are expected to continue this function for the now extended family system. Second siblings often do this easily in the normal flow of family events, but this task may become difficult in a marriage of two second siblings if either one or both have not clearly separated from their mother. Although they may be arguing about the issue, either directly or indirectly, neither can help the other understand the problem.

Third Siblings Married to Third Siblings

Third siblings thrive in a marriage in which both spouses are fully committed to the relationship, because they can focus on maintaining and balancing the relationship. Balance in relationships is very important to third siblings, and they constantly work to achieve it in their marriages.

The constant shifting and balancing of in-and-out patterns in the relationship is an accepted, if not acknowledged, part of a marriage between two third siblings. Sometimes, conflict arose about this issue in the marriage of Rex and Ruth, both third siblings, even though they understood it. In stressful situations, each wanted support from the other, but the other was not always available. At times, these psychological absences became issues of trust, and the pattern escalated into a vicious circle.

It was difficult for Ruth and Rex to make decisions because they moved in and out of the relationship and because each wanted to preserve as many choices as possible. Maneuvering to keep their choices open, both were often reluctant to commit themselves to some project or cause in the relationship. Although they were fully committed and loving in their marriage, each new enterprise seemed to be a new commitment. For example, if one of them was committed to the purchase of a new car, the other vacillated. If neither third sibling spouse is threatened psychologically, this pattern may be fully accepted. If the issues are not clear and one spouse is threatened, however, this kind of behavior may be interpreted as rejection or ambivalence about the value of the spouse or the marital relationship.

Because third siblings are relationship experts, Ruth and Rex could focus on the interactional patterns in their relationship and identify at least some of the issues. By focusing on the issues, however, they sometimes lost sight of the ideas, feelings, and implicit needs of the other.

Because of their ambivalence, third sibling spouses often accept a great deal of emotional abuse, inner turmoil, and confusion in a marriage. They tend to distort reality so that they can cling to the present situation until someone helps them conceptualize it more clearly by making connections to events, feelings, and marital issues. Without an adequate understanding that creates choices, they seem to be immobilized.

Although they usually have a complete understanding of the underlying principles, third siblings tend to ignore or simply fail to recall the details of an event. They often omit details from their description of events that their spouse has not attended, which may make the spouse feel excluded from sharing or fully knowing their experiences. In some contexts, third sibling spouses recognize that their spouses omit the details about a situation, identify this as an issue, and discuss it. Because the internal screening of data is such an integral part of the way in which third siblings make sense of their world, they are not always aware of their failure to reveal information important to their spouse. Consequently, they are often surprised when their spouse tells them that he or she feels excluded. The spouse who feels left out needs the information to stay connected in the context. If the well-being of the spouse is threatened, the information helps reestablish balance in the relationship.

Both partners bring their parents' marital issues and relationship rules into their own marriage. Because third siblings are experts on the marital relationship of their parents, they may impose the parental model on their own marriage. On the other hand, they may be determined that their marriage will not be like that of their parents.

Fourth Siblings Married to Fourth Siblings

The marital combination of two fourth siblings may be very productive. The spouses may work together on the same job or harmoniously apart with their respective responsibilities clear. If jobs are not completed, however, they feel responsible and urge their spouse to finish them, or they do the jobs themselves and become martyrs in the process.

Jack and Sally, two fourth siblings, had a great deal of expressed warmth and affection in their marriage. Socially, they liked and were comfortable with groups of friends, and there was little conflict over how many people to include in social activities. They both worked hard to keep their home peaceful and running smoothly. It was easy for them to work together democratically and to involve each other and their children in making decisions and completing projects.

Jack and Sally sometimes overwhelmed each other, partially because they had no one to help them perceive the world with more clarity. Because they each perceived the Gestalts and tended to see the beginning, middle, and end, with many pieces missing, they bogged down easily. They needed someone to break ideas, feelings, and behavior into smaller units. Their children occasionally did this for them.

Usually they were very supportive of each other. If one spouse believed that the other was being unfair and irresponsible, however, that spouse would subtly sabotage and undermine the other. As this occurred, primarily on the implicit level of awareness, and the spouse remained supportive on the explicit level, major confusion and dissonance resulted. All the implicit communication between the two was swept into their respective collections and accumulations, often creating enmeshment.

Enmeshment is a problem because fourth siblings have been trained to be system experts whose role is to maintain harmony in the system. Thus, in order to maintain harmony, Jack and Sally chose not to express what they saw as conflictual information or their personal wishes. Although they viewed themselves as powerless, they blamed themselves if problems developed in the system or if the other was in pain. Consequently, each did a great deal of mind reading and was overly responsible for the other. In times of crisis and stress, the emotions of one paralyzed the other, who did not know how to "fix it" and bring harmony into the system. In addition, both collected all the emotional "garbage" in the system and carried it as their own burden. The amount of garbage was compounded as they assumed each other's burdens.

Fourth siblings may bring into their marriage unresolved issues from their family of origin. If their family is and/or was dysfunctional, family members may expect fourth siblings to continue in their past roles (e.g., symptom bearer, scapegoat, or harmonizer). Their attempts to individuate and function in appropriate parental and spousal roles in their new family may precipitate crises of major proportions to draw the fourth sibling back into the extended family system.

If the extended family is having troubles, fourth siblings may immediately assume that they have failed in some way. In order to compensate for this, they may follow their childhood patterns and rush into the family system. This can create havoc for their spouse if the fourth sibling comes home with all the pain and debris and expects their spouse to cope with it. Both spouses are then overwhelmed with the debris and threats to their well-being. Each accepts the blame, and they "wallow" in it until it becomes a personal relationship issue that may surface in many arenas.

If both extended families experience problems at the same time, the burdens are multiplied. Couples may need outside help to sort out and relieve the pain and the accumulated feelings of blame for all that has happened.

CHAPTER 9

Intimacy, Communication, Decision Making, and Planning

Many factors influence interaction between people. Intimacy, communication, decision making, and planning are some of the factors that have the greatest growth and cause conflict in families.

Intimacy

A complex matter, intimacy is individualized for each marriage. In general, intimacy is a mutual feeling of personal closeness that accompanies the sharing of information, the sharing of feelings, the sharing of affection, and sexual intimacy. With the exception of sexual intimacy, these kinds of intimacy can be applied to all family relationships. The expression of intimacy varies with each family system and interpersonal subsystem, however.

Although everyone seeks some level of intimacy in relationships, many people develop fears with the anticipation of intimate experiences. The rewards of being close to another person must be balanced with the costs, and some individuals fear the costs will be too high. Perceived costs, such as being controlled, abandoned, or possessed by another, or losing a separate identity, often keep people from being close.

The expressions of intimacy and the needs and fears surrounding it are influenced by the themes, images, and boundaries of each person's family of origin. For example, an individual who grew up in a family that stressed the theme of shared feelings can identify emotions and share them with others. Images involve a person's self-perception in a particular role. A husband who sees himself as a nurturing, warm care-giver certainly communicates intimacy in a manner differently from that in which a husband who sees himself as a disciplinarian communicates intimacy. Boundaries govern how much intimacy can be shared within family subsystems and how much affection, information, and emotion can be shared with those outside the family system.

Thus, many factors influence a person's ability to be intimate with others. The rules that the family of origin has about being close, the ways in which feelings are shared, and the transmission of intimacy issues from the multigenerational family are some of the factors that affect an individual's expectations and feelings about intimacy in marriage. In addition, the characteristic response patterns of each sibling position influence the way in which individuals seek and provide intimacy, as well as their fears about being too close to another person.

First Children and Intimacy

First children are cautious about becoming too close to other people. They have the capacity to be intimate, but they need time. Because first children grow up with a sense of "never being good enough," they worry that other people will disapprove of them. Therefore, first children approach closeness in a relationship in a stepwise fashion, risking a little, waiting to see whether the other person approves, risking a little more, waiting to see if the other person still approves, until finally they discover that the relationship is safe. Then, they can risk sharing personal information.

First children have several fears that sometimes keep them from expressing and accepting intimacy in marriage. They fear being controlled by another person, which often prevents them from being totally involved in sexual encounters within the marriage. They also fear becoming a possession of another person and making themselves vulnerable to the disapproval of another. Their predominant focus on explicit information and analytical processes also hinders their expression of feelings. First children have difficulty understanding that simply sharing their feelings can create a form of intimacy. Because they cannot always explain their feelings rationally or logically, they have a tendency to invalidate what they feel for fear that, if they were to express their feelings, others would disapprove. Finally, their desire to produce interfaces with their fear of receiving disapproval and causes them to doubt whether they can be intimate in a "perfect" way.

The need of first children to be right may exacerbate intimacy issues. This need sometimes creates a barrier to sharing, because first children may initiate an argument if they sense that the other person believes them to be wrong. If the other person initiates any kind of touching when their defenses are high, first children may see the touching as an invasion of privacy and intrusion into their boundaries. Logic and analysis, coupled with an emphasis on explicit details, sometimes leads first children to use too many words, which further exaggerates any intimacy issues that may already be present. When a conflict about intimacy causes first children to feel threatened psychologically, they often withdraw, isolate themselves, and become unapproachable.

When other people accept first children and offer explicit praise for their expression of feelings, personal provision of information, and affectionate behavior, first children become more confident and less afraid to be intimate. In fact, they may even begin to believe that they can be "good enough." Learning that others can understand their feelings of inadequacy, first children experience a great relief. They learn that it is all right to be less than perfect, and they take themselves off probation with other people.

First children learn to be intimate by watching their father's relationship with their mother. If their father can share ideas and emotions, first children are likely to achieve intellectual and emotional intimacy with others. First siblings also learn intimacy from interacting with their mother in many of the same ways that their father does. They learn to be warm, caring, and affectionate when their father is warm, caring, and affectionate. If their father has unresolved issues about intimacy, however, these issues are likely to be transmitted to first children.

The characteristic response patterns for first siblings create both strengths and liabilities when these individuals try to form close, personal relationships with other people. Because first siblings like to share ideas and details, they can establish intellectual intimacy without too much difficulty. Furthermore, when they view their feelings as relevant to the attainment of some goal, first siblings can be very expressive of emotion as well. They approach even emotion through cognitive, analytical processes, however, and this can prove a barrier to intimacy. In addition, first siblings sometimes infringe on other people's rights by asking too many questions in their search for additional information. They are not always patient in waiting for the answers, which can irritate others and lead to a lack of intimacy.

As a result of their needs to be productive and independent, first siblings may not spend very much time with their spouse. They may become so involved with their work and other individual pursuits that they have no time to share activities with their spouse. In trying to be as productive as they think they should be, they begin to compartmentalize their world into pieces and may leave their spouse feeling neglected.

Second Children and Intimacy

In contrast to first children, second children draw close to other people relatively quickly. Because they recognize implicit cues from other people, second children sense the intimacy needs of others. Knowing intuitively the emotions that others are experiencing, often before the others are explicitly aware of them, second children work to help them share those emotions. Second children like to talk about ideas as well, but they cannot always express their ideas explicitly. Intellectual conversations often stimulate them to make their implicit, often vague ideas explicit, which allows them to make sense of these ideas and often leads to intellectual intimacy.

Because second children have difficulty delineating their personal boundaries, they sometimes fear closeness to another person. They worry that they may be engulfed by the other person as a result of their own tendency to blur identities and boundaries. Their sharing of emotions with another person may help separate their identity if the other person is clear about his or her personal boundaries and emotions. Second children often shy away from becoming close to a person who seems needy, however, for fear of melding with that person's pain and emptiness. If the other person has a great deal of implicit pain, second children may fear that they will have to take care of it; intimacy with such a person may make them feel used although they may not understand why.

Several factors may intensify these intimacy issues for second children. When they are confused by the incongruency between the explicit messages and the implicit structure, it is harder for them to be intimate. In addition, if second children feel that they have "lost their place" in the relationship, they appear irrational and confused. It is important for their spouse to assure second children that they have a place in the relationship. If they meld with the other person's ideas and emotions until they are not clear themselves who they are or what they want, they may be physically and emotionally close in a form of pseudo-intimacy.

Second children learn to be intimate from observing their mother's relationship with their father. They explicitly attend to their mother's behavior toward their father, but they also intuitively sense their mother's feelings about intimacy in her relationship with their father. In addition, second children learn to be intimate in their relationship with their older sibling, the first child. When second children are having difficulty with closeness, they often polarize to the cognitive mode. If this happens, the first child can reassure them that they have a place in the family. It also helps second children if someone can help them determine which of their feelings they have picked up from other people.

The strengths associated with the second sibling position in regard to intimacy lie in the ability of second siblings to express feelings warmly. Easily sensing personal issues in others, they respond with empathy and concern. They can help others sort out feelings because of their ability to focus on the implicit, underlying processes. Second siblings have problems with melding and flooding, however. If they are emotionally loaded with another's emotions, they have trouble establishing boundaries in sexual relationships (e.g., determining how close, how quickly, whether they have the right to refuse). If they are polarized, they may find it difficult to recognize their partner's nonverbal behavior and cues. Finally, second siblings often push for emotional intimacy before those in other sibling positions are ready. For example, first children often perceive the ability of a second child to read their implicitness as an intrusion into their privacy.

Third Children and Intimacy

Third children wait to see if the other person can be trusted to accept them as they are before they form a close relationship. Their needs to remain free and keep their choices open prevent instant closeness. Because of the in-and-out quality of third children, others often have difficulty determining whether third children want a close relationship or not. When they find someone they trust, however, third children can be warm, sensitive, and close in relationships.

The fear that third children have about intimacy centers on freedom and abandonment. Although third siblings want to be close at times, they also want the freedom to "go away" and operate from a detached position. They want to know that the other person will remain available while they are "out" psychologically. Third children fear being controlled by another person, as first children do, but their reasons differ. Third children want to keep their choices open and need always to be able to be separate. Sometimes, these needs keep them from ever committing themselves to a relationship.

Problems with intimacy can escalate when third children do not realize how much others care about them. Even though third siblings are the ones who go away psychologically, they wait for the other person in the relationship to reestablish connections, especially if the relationship is very important to them. If the other person never does so, third children begin to wonder whether the other person really cares about them. Any attempt by another person to take away their choices also intensifies intimacy problems for third children. They resist any effort to control them through power or authority for fear of losing their choices or being trapped. When third children are threatened by intimacy issues, they either fight or flee.

Other people can help third children with intimacy problems by validating their right to have choices. Rather than urging third children to make immediate decisions about relationships, others can help them explore their freedom. In addition, third children need to know that others will be available after third children have gone away. This knowledge helps third children to feel free to work out their issues without risking their relationships with other people. When they understand that other people will "be there," third children return to resume intimate behavior.

Third children learn to be intimate from the rules about closeness, sharing of ideas and feelings, and affection in their parents' marriage. When the parents have a healthy, loving sexual relationship, third children grow up with positive attitudes toward sexual expression. When the parents are close and can share both feelings and ideas to achieve emotional and intellectual intimacy, third children can be close to and open with others.

The desire of third siblings to make connections with other people is their primary strength in regard to intimacy. Also, when they are committed to a relationship, they are loyal friends who do not use personal information that the other person has disclosed against that other person. The greatest obstacle to intimacy for third siblings is their in-and-out behavior. When others do not understand this quality, they often give up trying to share feelings and to become close to third children.

Fourth Children and Intimacy

As in everything else, fourth children are impulsive in forming intimate relationships. They are spontaneous and willing to share their feelings and ideas. Because of their warmth and ease in establishing relationships, others usually enjoy the company of fourth children and want to be close to them.

The fears of fourth children that they will be overwhelmed by another person's emotions or their guilt if previous relationships have been disrupted may block intimacy. Because fourth children serve the role of trouble-shooters in their family or origin, they may form close relationships with others to minimize disruptions and create unity rather than to satisfy their own desire to be close. In this event, others often think the relationship is more intimate than it really is. If the other person is carrying a great deal of pain and tension, fourth children may either urge the other to do something or, if the pain is too great, withdraw. Neither of these responses creates feelings of closeness.

These intimacy issues are escalated for fourth children under several conditions. When they feel a powerful sense of duty to smooth over crises, but the personal cost of doing so seems too great, they may be immobilized. When others do not admit their feelings, fourth children become anxious because they cannot keep harmony in the system unless people accept and work to resolve their feelings. The ability of fourth children to participate in intimate exchanges in marriage is related to the amount of guilt and blame that they feel for problems in the relationship. If the other person does not accept part of the blame, for example, fourth children may become stubborn and avoid intimacy.

If threatened by intimacy issues, fourth children might appear flighty, heavy, or burdened.

If relationships in their family of origin are personal and close, fourth children learn to be intimate. If family members openly express their ideas and feelings, fourth children thrive. This is especially true when family members admit their feelings and express a great deal of affection and warmth. This kind of intimacy not only adds to family unity and harmony, but also assists fourth children in fulfilling their role assignment. Fourth children from such a family expect their relationships to be personal, close, and affectionate.

The impulsiveness of fourth siblings, coupled with their warmth and practice at trouble-shooting, facilitates their formation of close relationships with others. As a result of their family assignment to smooth over disruption in the system, however, fourth siblings may appear to be intimate when their feelings do not match their behavior. Their role in the family also creates a barrier to the honest sharing of their own feelings and thoughts. In sexual relationships, fourth siblings are sometimes so involved in trying to take care of the other person that they do not deal responsibly with their own feelings. Others find this dishonest and smothering at times.

Effects of Sibling Positions on Intimacy in Relationships

The characteristics of each of the four sibling positions in regard to intimacy, as summarized in Table 9–1, affect all relationships, as shown in the following examples.

Marital Combinations of First and Second Siblings

In the marriage of a first sibling to a second sibling, the first sibling's need to be right interfaces with the second sibling's need to have a place. At times, these two needs are in conflict. For example, the first sibling's dogmatic, analytical arguments may undermine the second sibling's place in the marriage. It is difficult for the second sibling spouse to initiate intimacy if he or she feels insecure about having a place. Similarly, it is difficult for the first sibling spouse to respond intimately when he or she is stuck in "rightness."

This marital combination can achieve intellectual intimacy, provided that the second sibling spouses are not polarized in emotion and provided that they do not fight with their first sibling spouse about whose facts are more correct or whose argument is more logical. If the second siblings are polarized into emotionality, the first sibling spouse perceives this position as irrational and too emotional. Furthermore, the first sibling assumes that the second sibling has not considered the facts.

Table 9–1 Intimacy and sibling positions.

Intimacy variables	Sibling positions			
	1	2	3	4
Development of intimacy	Slow, cautiously	Quickly	Slow, cautiously	impulsively
Obstacles in intimacy	Fear of being controlled by another, being owned by others, being vulnerable to disapproval	Blurred boundaries, fear of being engulfed	Fear of loss of freedom, being controlled, being engulfed, abandonment	Fear of being overwhelmed by guilt and pain
Source of knowledge about intimacy	Father's relationship to mother, father's relationship to first	Mother's relationship to father, second's relationship to first	Intimacy rules of parents' marriage relationship	Intimacy in the family
Intimacy issues	Can I be vulnerable, independent, adequate? If I share information and feelings, will others still approve of me?	Can I be separate? Is this really for me? Am I being used?	Can I be intimate and still have my choices? Can I go away and come back? Can I be separate?	Will there be too much pain or guilt? Am I doing it to take care of someone?
Causes of escalation in intimacy issues	Sense of others' disapproval; need to be analytical, right; wordiness	Confusion, lost sense of place, enmeshment, unacknowledged feelings of others	Loss of choices, failure of others to acknowlege that they care	Sense of duty, unacknowledged feelings of others, amount of guilt
Evidence of escalated intimacy	Withdrawal and stoney look	Confusion and hurt	Flight or fight	Flighty or heavily burdened appearance
Resolution of intimacy issues	Others' expression of approval and explicit praise	Actual closeness without melding	Validation of right to have choices, availability of others	Others' acceptance of part of blame and notice that what they do is important
Therapy issues	Sharing of feelings, acceptance of feedback, surrender of control	Inappropriate care-giving, establishment of boundaries	Need to understand their going away & be explicit about coming back	Inappropriate care-giving and being responsible in a more direct way

This sibling combination may find it difficult to achieve emotional intimacy for a number of reasons. First siblings tend to be focused more on cognitive processes than on emotional ones, whereas the opposite is true for second siblings. First siblings may see their second sibling spouse's reading of their underlying feelings as an invasion of their privacy and boundaries. The attempt to make the implicit feelings of first siblings explicit creates a fear in them that their spouse is trying to control them. This confrontation also appears to be an indictment of their performance to first children. They respond by denying what their second sibling spouse senses, leading the spouse to sense greater incongruency. The patterns compound to more confusion for both spouses.

The tendency of second siblings to meld with their marriage partner interfaces with their first sibling spouse's desire to be independent. The melding scares the first sibling, who cannot understand what has happened on an explicit level, becomes confused, and backs away. As the first sibling moves away, the second sibling senses a loss of place in the relationship and becomes confused as well.

First sibling spouses worry about their performance and seek information from their spouse about their sexual response. First siblings can be sexually pushy, which interfaces with the boundary issues of second siblings about whether they can set rules about the context in which sexual behavior occurs.

Intimacy between Third and Fourth Adolescent Siblings

Issues of intimacy also surface in relationships between siblings in the same family. In the relationship of a 10-year-old sibling and a 13-year-old third sibling in the same family, for example, the interface between the fourth sibling's impulsiveness and spontaneity and the third sibling's tentativeness and in-and-out behavior may sometimes result in playfulness. The fourth sibling's spontaneity may fulfill the third sibling's need to be connected. At other times, however, the third sibling may need to be detached and on the periphery of the interaction. In this situation, the third sibling may see the impulsiveness of the fourth sibling as inappropriate and pestering. The fourth sibling may be rebuffed by the third sibling's psychological absence and be very surprised when the third sibling psychologically reenters the relationship, acting as if nothing has ever changed.

Fourth siblings experience this constant in-and-out behavior of third siblings as disruptive at times. They may harass their third siblings over unity and harmony issues. These arguments hinder the capacity of these siblings to share information, emotions, and affection. Fourth siblings also harass third siblings when their parents' marriage is poor, and this blocks their ability to have an intimate relationship.

Communication

Relationships are created, maintained, changed, and destroyed by communication. People are the communicators, and the variations in the ways that people communicate reflect their past experience, particularly family experience. Therefore, it follows that each sibling position develops unique communication characteristics.

First Children and Communication

Because first children focus on details of situations, they are most likely to communicate to others what they can observe, the properties of people or things. They often provide too much verbal detail, and other people become lost or overwhelmed in trying to keep up with the elaborate descriptions.

The analytical style with which first children approach life makes it difficult for them to understand implicit messages. They see intuition as magical and discount it because it is not logical and does not focus on facts. Similarly, because first children often see emotions and feelings as irrational, they tend to discount not only the feelings of other people, but also their own feelings.

The way in which people deal with their own feelings and the feelings of other people is an important part of communication, however. First children deal with the feelings of other people by trying to connect them to events that should logically elicit such feelings; this is an analytical process. If first children can find no rational basis for the other person's feelings, they may try to change the other's feelings on the basis of logic. First children may not even express their own emotions if they believe that such an expression of feelings will be met with disapproval from others. Their need to be right is greater than is their need to express feelings.

First children approach their world by trying to understand parts of a context. A lack of information and the presence of too many parts block communication for first children. Their communication also becomes ineffective when they assume that someone important to them disapproves of what they have done. In these instances, first children intentionally omit information or distort events in order to present themselves as efficient and productive to the other person.

Other people help first children resolve these communication problems by providing sufficient information and by being explicit about their approval of what first children do. When bogged down in too many details, first children need to be reminded that it is not necessary for them to do everything by themselves. This is often a revelation to first children; they are relieved to accept the help, but they would never have thought of requesting assistance. It is also helpful to first children for others to remind them that they do not have to be perfect. When first children realize that others will accept them even when they are not productive, they will communicate more openly.

Second Children and Communication

Second children focus on implicit messages within the underlying structure of the communication context. In a social context, second children know how people feel, even if those people never talk about their feelings. Their attention to the implicit causes second children to be very sensitive to metacommunication. They receive and respond to implicit messages much more readily than do first children, and they are often aware of the metalevel even when the sender of the message is not. Second children have a sense of incongruency between verbal and nonverbal communication, and between the explicit and implicit messages and themes in human relationships. Their style is affective. First, they sense emotionally what is happening in a given context; then they try to force the implicit to the surface in order to add clarity to communication.

Incongruency is the greatest hindrance to communication for second children. When messages at the implicit level are very different from messages at the explicit level, second children try to clarify the discrepancies. If this attempt at clarification fails, second children cannot make sense of their perceptions and become confused. This prevents them from communicating effectively. The tendency of second children to meld with the feelings of others and flood with emotion is another barrier to communication. These two processes result in a lack of clarity in communication.

Second children can become better communicators by learning to make their implicit processes more explicit. In doing so, they learn not to assume that others know what they know and are thinking. By acknowledging their own incongruencies, others validate the ways in which second children make sense of their world and increase the clarity of communication.

Third Children and Communication

Third children notice connections between parts. Their process is primarily cognitive in that they try to understand the principles on which things operate. Third children learn which principles apply to various social contexts, but they may omit the details.

Third children use both explicit and implicit information to arrive at their conclusions, but their process relies primarily on explicit information. They make their observations, go away and think about different ways of connecting their observations, and return with a new perspective. Their ability to provide a new perspective is a great benefit to effective communication.

Third children deal with feelings from a detached, cognitive position. They step out of the interactional communication process to study the linkage between their own and the other's emotions, they examine the ways in which emotions are linked to events in the transactional process. When they have sorted through emotions in this way, they reenter the two-way communication channel. At this point, they may decide to express the relevant emotions and link them to their own and the other's behaviors, or they may keep their understanding of the processes to themselves. Their action depends largely on how much the other person needs to engage in a two-way process to bring closure to the communication.

If third children do not understand the context in which communication occurs, they cannot find the underlying principles and do not communicate efficiently. Without confidence in their perception of the underlying principles, they proceed with communication cautiously and tentatively. At this point, they do not need explanations about the attributes of the parts, but rather they need assistance in understanding the relationships of the parts to each other.

When third children have communication problems, other people can help in two ways. First, other people need to provide alternatives and choices as they communicate with third children. The use of absolute words, such as "always," "never," "must," "on every occasion," creates communication obstacles for third children; they realize that such words do not apply to every context. Second, others can talk about the ways in which events are related or connected, rather than the events themselves. Focusing on what people did, what people said, and how things looked helps third children to see these connections.

Fourth Children and Communication

Fourth children see the whole before they see the parts. They learn to break things into parts, but they can make sense of the parts only as they fit into the whole. Their approach to the whole is first affective and later cognitive. In other words, they have an immediate, impulsive reaction to situations. They cannot always explain their affective response, which makes it appear that their focus is implicit. In fact, the focus of fourth children is probably more implicit than explicit, but it is both. It is implicit in the sense that they feel responsible for others' emotions; it is explicit in the sense that they know who has the emotions.

Fourth children are capable of handling their own and other people's feelings in explicit ways. In most cases, they can label and express their feelings.

The one drawback to their communication style is that they tend to try to take care of other people's feelings by not being fully honest or expressive of their own. They consider unity and harmony more important than the expression of their own feelings.

Fourth children experience communication breakdown when the whole of something is too large, when someone else's affect is too intense, or when they cannot see how the parts (i.e., beginning, middle, and end) are related to the whole. In each of these conditions, fourth children become overwhelmed and distort communication. Others can help fourth children communicate more clearly by acknowledging their own feelings, by reassuring the fourth children that they are not responsible for these feelings, and by breaking down the whole into smaller parts.

Effects of Sibling Positions on Communication in Relationships

In communication, all four approaches of the various sibling positions complement each other (see Table 9–2). They each add clarity to the communication of meaning.

Marital Combinations of Second and Third Siblings

Although third siblings focus on connections and second siblings focus on the underlying messages, their approaches are complementary in some respects. Third siblings try to make connections explicit in their attempts to understand underlying principles, and second siblings try to make the implicit explicit. Because the implicit contains many connections, the role of second siblings facilitates the understanding of third siblings.

Third siblings tend to approach the world primarily through cognition, identifying and expressing feelings only secondarily. If second siblings are polarized to the cognitive pole, they also approach situations through cognition. If they are polarized to the affective pole, however, their third sibling spouse may have difficulty understanding the implicitness of their emotional process. To the third sibling spouse, it may appear that the second sibling is irrational, that he or she has made too many assumptions, and that these assumptions have no connections to events that should logically precipitate such emotions. The third sibling may be confused and frustrated by the second sibling's melding, as the second sibling may be unable to make the melding process explicit. After all, if second siblings could make the implicit explicit, they would not meld nearly as often.

When third siblings detach themselves from a relationship and move to an introspective position, their second sibling spouse may become confused

Table 9-2 Communication and sibling positions.

Communication variables	Sibling positions			
	1	2	3	4
Focus	Details, cognitive	Underlying messages, affective or cognitive	Connections, cognitive	Gestalt, affective
Formation of meaning	Parts to wholes	Parts to wholes	Connections among parts	Whole, then parts
Implicit versus explicit focus	Explicit	Implicit or explicit	More explicit	More implicit
Resolution of block in communication	Giving information without punishing	Making the implicit explicit	Providing connections	Breaking the whole into parts
Dealing with own and other people's feelings	Cognition	Efforts to make implicit feelings explicit	Cognitive, detached position to sort through feelings	Explicit affect, but efforts to smooth over feelings

because the in-and-out behavior of the third siblings seems incongruent. In an attempt to force the apparent discrepancy into the open, the second sibling may restrict the third sibling's range of choices. The third sibling's response of either fighting intensely or moving away even more often increases the second sibling's confusion. It is likely that neither spouse can communicate about this interactional process without outside intervention.

First and Fourth Sibling Combinations in Grandparent-Grandchild Relationships

Grandchildren who are fourth siblings are likely to think that their grand-parents who are first siblings talk too much and use words that are too big. Focusing first on the Gestalt and then on the parts only if the relationship of the parts to the whole is apparent, the grandchildren may see some of the details of the grandparents' conversation as irrelevant and confusing. If the grandparents' explanations help the fourth sibling grandchildren see how the "beginning, middle, and end" work together to achieve some purpose, however, the grandchildren find the conversation relevant and interesting—provided that the detail of the grandparents' communication does not overwhelm the grandchildren.

The immediate impulsiveness of the fourth sibling grandchildren is probably pleasurable for the first sibling grandparents when the grandchildren are young. As this impulsiveness continues into adolescence, however, the grand-parents begin to see the grandchildren as somewhat irrational, with a tendency to overreact emotionally. If there is tension in the nuclear family of the grandchildren, the grandparents may not understand the guilt and blame that the fourth sibling grandchildren feel. In response, the grandchildren behave and communicate in ways that smooth over the tensions of their grandparents, who experience the care-giving as pleasant and enjoyable. If the pain or tension in the family is so great that the grandchildren cause trouble, however, first sibling grandparents are likely to discount such feelings and behavior as irrational and unfounded.

First sibling grandparents can be very helpful in teaching their fourth sibling grandchildren to break down the whole into parts. This strategy is particularly useful in the grandchildren's schoolwork.

Decision Making and Planning

First Children, Decision Making, and Planning

First children have a great deal of practice in making decisions. They are accustomed to being central in their family of origin, and they want to be seen as involved contributors. Their strength in making decisions is in their ability to sort out details and make everything explicit. For example, they are good at listing advantages and disadvantages, and at gathering the information necessary to make a decision. In general, first children are good decision makers, but they worry excessively about whether their decisions are right and whether others will approve. They often want others to make minor decisions. This relieves them of the responsibility for the correctness of the decision. They are blocked in making decisions that require information from others because they feel and act as if they must do everything by themselves, including making decisions.

First children love to plan, and they often construct detailed lists of the steps that are needed to accomplish a task. They may never complete the steps, however. Similarly, they prefer to have someone else they trust implement their solutions to problems. This pattern is often very frustrating to their non-first sibling spouse, who expects them to do what they plan. Although it seems contradictory, this lack of follow-through is related to first children's needs for productivity warring against their needs for approval. Consequently, planning can be fun and fruitful, whereas to carry out the plan exposes the results and the first siblings to criticism and rejection. If first children sense that the product being planned is expected by someone else, however, they become very results oriented and do not stop until the job is done. They also tend to complete tasks if they personally want the finished product or outcome.

Second Children, Decision Making, and Planning

Second children have no difficulty in making decisions, provided that there are few incongruencies in the situation. If there is some confusion about what is expected, or if there is more than one message about who is responsible for various aspects of the decision, second children are uncomfortable. Sometimes, they know intuitively that something about a decision is not quite right, but they cannot make the problem explicit.

If second children are polarized to the cognitive pole, they are very much like first children in their ability to list details, gather information, and set deadlines for decisions. If they are polarized to the affective pole, they approach decision-making processes emotionally, switching back and forth between alternatives. Eventually, they make a decision just to get out of this situation, but they may not secure enough explicit information on which to base their decision; it becomes an emotional preference.

Second children like to be involved in planning, as it gives them a special place. Furthermore, they are good at providing an underlying structure into which the details can fit. When planning a project that involves several people, they make sure that all participants know what their responsibilities are so that no implicit expectation can cause confusion. Second children also have an intuitive sense of others' feelings about the decisions being made and the process. They attempt to make these feelings explicit, which usually helps others feel good about the process and the resulting decisions.

Third Children, Decision Making, and Planning

Third children often appear ambivalent about making decisions. If a decision limits their choices, third children feel threatened. If they think they are being forced to make a decision, they may become rebellious and stubborn. They are good decision makers when they decide to be, however, because they can make connections between details and see perspectives that those in other sibling positions overlook.

Third children are aware of the rules of the decision-making process, and they make these rules explicit so that everyone understands them. They are concerned about who should be included in making the decisions, who should be excluded, and what the issues are. If the rules for decision making are drastically different from those employed in their parents' marriage, third children are uncomfortable and want to change the rules. Sometimes, third children make decisions independently, especially when they have moved to the periphery of a relationship to study issues, and have sorted out their feelings, observations, and ideas. This introspective process prevents others from understanding the basis on which third children make decisions.

Third children are good people to have involved in planning. They help others see how to get from point to point; in other words, they provide the sequencing, the linkages. Moreover, they can apply principles that they have learned in other contexts to the context under consideration. Sometimes, however, third children get bogged down in their tentativeness about plans. In an effort to keep their choices open, they can be vague in details or in their commitment to a plan.

Fourth Children, Decision Making, and Planning

Because their family role assignment is to support others, thus bringing harmony and unity to the system, fourth children are more comfortable than are their siblings in having other people make decisions, provided that the other people consider their input. They also tend to like democratic decision-making processes, because everyone is involved, including themselves. Fourth children may not make their own input into the decision very clear, however. They are implicitly aware of others' feelings about the decision, the process, and the group, and they can become more interested in making the process run smoother than in having their own input recognized.

In planning, fourth children need to see the beginning, the middle, and the end of what they are planning. Otherwise, it appears to them that all the parts lack purpose. Fourth children contribute to planning by helping others to connect the parts and see their overall purpose. When fourth children plan alone, their plans are often not detailed. They understand what their plan is supposed to accomplish, but they may not understand how to break the task into steps so that they can proceed. If they do plan the steps, the activities associated with each step may be vague.

Effects of Sibling Positions on Decision Making and Planning in Relationships

Clearly, the characteristic patterns of decision making and planning for each of the sibling positions, as shown in Table 9–3, affect relationships.

Marital Combinations of Second and Fourth Siblings

When working together to make decisions, fourth sibling spouses help second sibling spouses to be more explicit by encouraging them to acknowledge their own feelings and to process events. Unlike fourth siblings, second siblings are not usually expressive about their likes and dislikes, although they may have an intuitive grasp of them. Sometimes, second siblings recognize implicitly that there is something wrong with a decision, but they cannot identify it. Because fourth siblings have practice at trouble-shooting and identifying disruptions, they can assist their second sibling spouse in determining the cause of such reaction.

At times, second and fourth sibling spouses placate each other in the decision-making process. The fourth sibling spouse is willing to pay the personal price in order to maintain peace and harmony, and the second sibling spouse has always taken care of people; therefore, they function the same way in decision-making contexts. At a later time, both may be angry that they have done this, but they still have a tendency to take care of each other's underlying processes rather than to admit their feelings about the decision itself.

In planning, second and fourth sibling marital combinations can be very creative. The implicitness of the second sibling spouse and the impulsiveness of the fourth sibling spouse combine to form a perspective that neither has really considered in the past. On the other hand, they sometimes have difficulty

Table 9–3 Decision making, planning, and sibling positions.

Intimacy variables	Sibling positions			
	1	*2*	*3*	*4*
Decision-making issues	Need to be right, desire to be central and to have own way	Decisions as burden if there are conflicting messages about who has power and responsibility, emotional reaction to decisions, implicit disagreement	Need to keep choices open, make decisions independently	Acceptance of others' decisions, if their input is considered
Planning issues	Plans, but no follow-through	Plans disrupted by incongruencies	Difficulty with commitment	Inability to break whole into specific parts

confirming their assumptions about the plan or the process. Second siblings make assumptions and act on them without making them explicit, sometimes without even being aware that they have made such assumptions. Fourth siblings are prone to behave similarly because of their impulsiveness.

Second and fourth sibling spouses share the ability to process what is sensed by both of them in the planning context, and that helps the second sibling spouses to make explicit the parts of the situation with many details overlooked by fourth siblings. The emphasis of fourth siblings on making the separate steps and parts fit the overall purpose assists second siblings in making their implicit, intuitive ideas become a purposeful part of the plan.

Marital Combinations of First and Third Siblings

Both first and third siblings tend to do much planning and research before presenting their ideas to their spouses. First sibling spouses get as much information as possible about all of the variables relevant to making a decision. They visit libraries, check with experts, and get as many details as they can. Armed with this unshared information, they select four or five different variations of the same theme and present them to their spouses in an attempt to get their approval. Being third siblings, the spouses are fairly ambivalent and tentative about what they want. In what appears as ambivalence and tentativeness to their spouses, third sibling spouses explore the larger picture of alternatives, going away into introspection to do so. This confuses first siblings who become frustrated and angry because they perceive their spouses tentativeness as disapproval of their efforts. Nevertheless, they continue to search for more details and alternatives. Third sibling spouses react in frustration because their spouses have not stated their preferences and appear to be forcing the third sibling spouses to make a decision.

The plans mutually developed by first and third sibling spouses are generally very thorough and creative. When they work together comfortably with mutual goals, third sibling spouses provide more connections and a larger perspective for the plan than do first siblings. Utilizing the details and careful research provided by their first sibling spouses, third sibling spouses spark creativity that employs both their strengths.

CHAPTER *10*

Sibling Issues in Single-Parent Families and Step-Families

The characteristics associated with the four basic sibling positions affect not only the nuclear family with two parents and their children living together in the same household, but also different family forms such as single-parent families and step-families.

Transitions in Family Form

Many single-parent families and step-families begin as nuclear families. Consequently, sibling subsystems generally begin in a nuclear family. As family structures are modified, the transitions through which the family must pass are likely to affect sibling position patterns.

The first transition is from the nuclear family to the single parent family, most commonly because of widowhood or divorce. The death of a spouse causes a major change in the membership structure of the household. The family becomes a single-parent family for an indefinite period of time, perhaps permanently. Divorce requires the family to pass through a transition from a nuclear family to a binuclear family (see Figure 10–1), in which the two parents in the nuclear family become single parents, set up separate households, and maintain some kind of contact, usually motivated through concern for their children (Ahrons, 1981).

The family trauma and emotional stress caused by a divorce are similar to those caused by the death of a spouse. Each event reduces the parent subsystem to a single parent. Like some of those who are widowed, some divorced

127

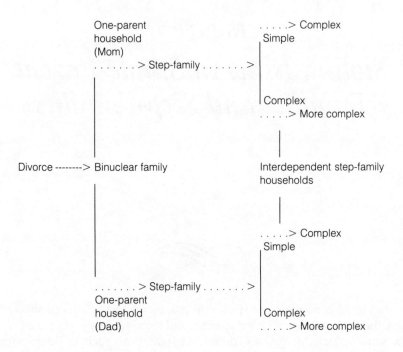

Figure 10–1 Family transitions: Divorce to binuclear family to step-families.

parents never remarry. The mother-run, single-parent household is the predominant form of the divorced family in the United States. It is also the one most often encountered in mental health settings (Glenwick & Mowerey, 1986).

The second transition occurs when single parents remarry and create a step-family. Step-families move through a variety of transitions, from the simple to the complex to the more complex. The degree of complexity is determined by the number of sibling subsystems. In the simple step-family, a single parent marries someone who has no children, thus establishing a sibling subsystem that is composed of either "her" children or "his" children, and a parent subsystem that is composed of one parent and a step-parent.

The complex step-family has two sibling subsystems, one with "her" children and one with "his" children. In addition, it has a parent subsystem that consists of a parent and a step-parent for each sibling subsystem. The step-family may also be considered complex if it includes either "her" or "his" children, but not both, and "our" children. Whether both sibling subsystems live in the same household or in separate households and visit regularly or sporadically, the interactions of the two sibling subsystems with parents and step-parents, and with each other, create a complex step-family system.

The step-family structure is more complex when the marriage of two single parents produces "our" children, adding a third sibling subsystem to the family. The parents in the home now serve many parental roles. In addition, two other sets of parents may be involved if the father of "her" children and the mother of "his" children have remarried. Combinations of single parents and deceased parents also add to the confusion. If children are added to the other step-families, the sibling subsystems become very complex indeed. Each child in each subsystem has a sibling position that interacts with those in the other sibling subsystems, leading to competition and confusion about job assignments.

Regardless of motives, desires, and feelings toward ex-spouses, the two step-family households form an interdependent alliance. The planning of schedules, the exchange of information, and the competition for economic and personal resources require some degree of communication and reliance on the other.

Complexity of Family Membership Changes

Transitions from one family form to another always involve shifts of family membership. When these shifts occur, patterns of response for sibling positions interact with family membership issues and create some observable dynamics.

Family membership units of spouses, parents, and siblings are affected by the transitions to other family forms (see Table 10–1). When a spouse dies, for example, the remaining spouse loses a marital companion permanently. Although the remaining spouse may remarry, he or she is never really free of the history of the relationship with the original companion. The parent subsystem is affected by the permanent absence of one parent, either because of death or a decision to have little or no contact with the family; by the decision to co-parent from separate households; and by the addition of step-parents. Sibling subsystems are affected by the changes in the parent subsystem. They are also affected by the deletions in the sibling subsystem that occur when siblings are divided between two households and by the addition of step-children and half-siblings. Additions to the sibling subsystems may duplicate sibling positions and cause conflict.

Children and parents in single-parent families and step-families may have problems associated with loyalty to absent parents. It is as if the ghosts of the absent parents remained in the home to remind each sibling and the remaining parent that the absent parents are still connected to the family. Whether the

Table 10–1 Family membership changes.

Members affected	Single parent/ family death	Single parent/ family divorce	Step-family
Spouse	Permanent loss of that companion	Permanent loss of that companion	Replacement of that companion
Parent	Permanent loss of one parent	Loss of one parent's daily contact, possibility of sharing parents	Same as single/divorced; addition of step-parent, possibly as a parental replacement
Sibling Subsystem	Usually not changed in membership	May be split permanently or temporarily	Subsystems added, split, and shared

absent parents are dead or living in some other place, the loyalty of family members intermingles with feelings of hurt, anger, and loss. If these feelings are not made explicit, they may surface from time to time, even when the children are adults, depending on the situation and the degree of dysfunction for the individual. Although loyalty may cause problems in sibling subsystems in step-families, most of such problems arise in parent-child and step-parent-child relationships.

The number of members in step-family households is variable because of additions and deletions of parents and siblings. Visits of children who live in other households, as well as the presence of extended family members and/or unrelated people who live with the family, add to the confusion and affect the stability of sibling position roles.

Membership Changes in Single-Parent Families

The loss of a parent by death or divorce not only immediately affects the number and kind of resources available to a family, but also changes the family structure and processes. For example, Dan Brown was killed in a car accident five years ago, leaving a wife, Andrea, and three children: Cynthia, then 12, now 17; Tom, then 10, now 15; and Christopher, then 7, now 12 years of age (see Figure 10–2). Insurance allowed Andrea to obtain special training, and she now works five days a week as a computer programmer. Although she dates, she is not seriously considering remarriage.

The major membership issue for the Brown family was the loss of a valued family member, a loving husband, and a kind father. His death did not change the membership of the sibling subsystem, but the family roles of the remaining

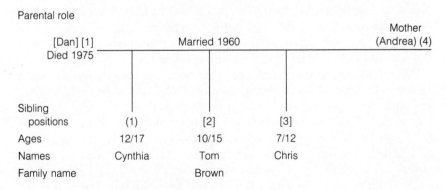

Figure 10–2 Single-parent family: The Browns.

family members had to be modified to compensate for the loss of a family member who performed certain roles himself.

Binuclear families experience the loss of a parent from the household, but the family membership issues are different. The reality of the missing parent is manifested through events such as personal contacts, the visits of children, conflict over resources, and wishes of family members. In spite of these differences, the dynamics of loss and grieving, rule and role structure changes, sibling position responses, and adjustment are much the same.

Membership Changes in Step-Families

The membership structure of the step-family system varies with the individual family and is usually very complex. It is also very dynamic because of blurred sibling roles of children born in the family, duplicated sibling roles within the same system, missing sibling roles, and the repeated addition and deletion of sibling roles because of visits (see Table 10–2). Relationships become very complex, as step-families combine step-siblings with half-siblings and full-siblings. This complexity is always a factor in step-family functioning.

His or Hers and Ours

In the Greely step-family, a traditional family has become a complex family system (see Figure 10–3). At first, there was only one step-parent with only one sibling subsystem. Alex brought three children from a previous marriage (i.e., Sally, 13; Bill, 11; and Kevin, 8) to his new marriage with Susan. The primary residence of these children is with their father. Their mother resides in another state, so they visit her during holidays and school vacations. Susan had never been married before and had no children. She was step-mother to Alex's three children for three years before she had her first child. Sibling position assignments and roles during this time remained the same as they had been in the nuclear family, although Susan's expectations may have been different from those of the children's biological mother.

When Kane and Tod were born to Susan and Alex, the previously existing sibling roles blurred their sibling position roles; that is, their roles have characteristics of more than one sibling position pattern. Although Susan may have accepted and loved her step-children, her anticipation and expectations for her own children are for first and second children. Alex, on the other hand, already had three children. Although he was as excited and pleased about the births of Kane and Tod as he had been about the births of his first three children, his expectations for the children in his new family are for fourth and fifth children. Furthermore, Alex's children view the new arrivals as younger

Table 10–2 Blurred, duplicated, or missing sibling position roles in step-families.

Sibling position roles	Most affected system/subsystem	Stability	Productivity	Parents
Blurred/blended roles	Sibling subsystems, sometimes issues of favoritism by parents of step-siblings	Compromise of roles to please both parents and family; stabilization of system in functional family	Increased productivity and new products possible with blended roles; if family dysfunctional, slow and impeded production	Some parental friction if first set of siblings are successful in triangulating parents
Duplicated roles	Step-sibling subsystem that has duplicate role	Disruptive fighting, whether implicit or explicit; occurrence of fighting whether step-family is functional or dysfunctional	Results reduced by fighting; if cooperating, very productive	Parents often triangulated over rules, expectations, and values
Missing roles	Remaining parent and siblings from nuclear family system	Sense of loss, leading to behavior that upsets the step-family system	Job assignments not filled, disruptive until adjustments are made; the more dysfunctional the family the longer the adjustment period	Parent of missing children grieving and guilt-ridden; disruptive to marital and other parent-child relationships

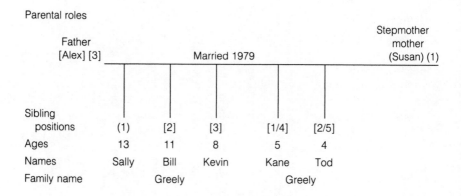

Figure 10–3 Step-family: The Greelys.

siblings. As a result of their blurred sibling positions, Kane and Tod receive mixed messages about their role in the family. The strongest message about their functional family system roles comes from the size of the system and the needs of its members. Because the first three roles were filled, for example, Kane's role assignment is that of a fourth sibling—to be responsible for the unity and harmony of the family.

The size and needs of the family environment also shape the perceptual orientation of the two new children. Therefore, Kane perceives the world as complex and holistic much as any other fourth child perceives it. The story for Tod is more indefinite, partly because less is known about the patterns of children after the fourth position. He may receive messages from the system for productivity and performance much like the messages that the first child receives. There is no way that his perceptual orientation replicates that of the first sibling, however, because the system in which he lives is so complex.

The mixed messages from the family affect the self-esteem and well-being sibling patterns for Kane and Tod. Their parents send them different messages about their position in the family, although neither of them is necessarily negative or conflictual. For example, Susan has expectations for her first child, Kane, that do not match Alex's expectations for his fourth child. Alex has already expended his first child expectations on Sally.

The family is more complex with three sibling subsystems: (1) the full siblings from the father's first marriage—Sally, Bill, and Kevin; (2) the full siblings from father's second marriage, to Susan—Kane and Tod; and (3) the half-sibling subsystem created by joining the two subsystems. Although this type of step-family is less complicated than is a step-family that includes unrelated sibling subsystems, close observation is needed to determine the ways in which self-esteem is developed and nourished, as well as the ways in which each sibling reacts to psychological threats.

Sibling subsystems are affected the most by blurred sibling position roles. Questions of favoritism are often raised. For example, the older Greely children may accuse Susan, their step-mother, of favoring her own children. If they want attention from their father and he seems involved with Susan and the younger children, they may accuse him of "not caring about us anymore." If the children can triangulate the parents in this way, friction may develop in the marital relationship. Because the younger children are the older children's half-siblings, however, they quickly form the usual brother and sister relationship with them. In a functional step-family, most of the friction about favoritism either subsides or comes to resemble that in nuclear families.

The blurring of two sibling positions is for parents an implicit compromise that works to stabilize the family system. The naturalness of the entrance into the family system of the two younger children (i.e., through birth) encourages an accommodation and utilization of their sibling roles for the productive needs of the system. This occurs quite smoothly, without disruption or competition.

His and Hers

The blending of families that occurs when two single parents marry creates a very common step-family system. In the Williams household, Barbara's children (the Millers), are older than Jon's (see Figure 10–4). Therefore, the family must deal with both adolescents and young children in regard to parent-child relationships, different family names, and duplicated sibling positions.

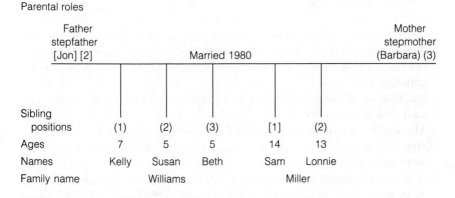

Parental roles						
Father stepfather [Jon] [2]			Married 1980			Mother stepmother (Barbara) (3)
Sibling positions	(1)	(2)	(3)	[1]	(2)	
Ages	7	5	5	14	13	
Names	Kelly	Susan	Beth	Sam	Lonnie	
Family name		Williams		Miller		

Figure 10–4 Step-family: The Williams.

The duplicate sibling roles in this step-family have the most effect on the two step-sibling subsystems (see Table 10- 3). Sam, 14 years old, and Kelly, 7 years old, are both first siblings, born into two different family environments. Because Sam is 7 years older and bigger than Kelly, much of their competition for the first sibling role was subtly camouflaged. Kelly tattled on Sam, for example, and even made up stories about him occasionally to tell his mother or her father. Taking his centrality for granted, Sam was unaware of any competition; he viewed Kelly as a little kid who liked to make trouble.

Now that the initial fighting about job assignments has been completed, Sam and Kelly are both very helpful to the productivity of the family system. Because of their age difference, it was possible to work out noncompetitive assignments for specific tasks. They insist on doing the interpersonal tasks in their own way, however, especially in taking care of each individual in their own family subsystem. Sam and Kelly may wear the rest of the family down with their bossing, their endless arguments centered on the right way to do things, and their predictable attempts to triangulate Barbara and Jon into the fray. The rules, expectations, and values of each parent cause confusion; until they are made explicit and family members know which ones are to be honored, which ones have been discarded, and what new ones have been installed, the battles and misunderstandings will go on throughout the family. Loyalties to absent parents also cloud sibling and parent-child interactions.

Susan and Beth are twins who are much younger than their step-siblings. Being twins, they have already made some accommodation in role sharing. Susan and Lonnie, both second siblings, are concerned about having a unique place in the family. This was more of an issue at first; all of them have now sorted out their places in the newly created environment.

His, Hers, and Ours

When children from two single-parent families are joined in a step-family and children are born to that family, blurred, duplicated, and missing sibling roles are part of the family system. Family relationships become very complex in this family.

In the Meyers' household, Tom had brought Jerry, his first child, to live with Peggy and her 4 children (see Figure 10–5). Tom's 11-year-old second son lives with his mother in another step-family in the same city. He is a missing sibling in the first Meyers family; consequently, his absence affects his father and brother more than it affects the rest of this step-family. The tasks that Eddie performed independently and with his father and brother are still missed in their subsystem; the longer that Eddie is out of the family on a daily basis, however, the less his contribution is missed. Each time Eddie comes to visit his

Table 10–3 Duplicate role interaction in sibling position patterns.

Sibling positions	Family roles	Perceptual orientation	Identity/ well-being
1–1	Fights about whose rules to follow and who is more right; loyalty issue involved with the rules	Possible involvement in long, wordy, rational arguments because of focus on details and semantics	Competition for centrality, need to be right, sense of insecurity
2–2	Unknowing cooperation by giving emotional support to family members; confusion for siblings in the same family subsystem; sometimes disloyal appearance	Polarities that complement or cause emotional entanglement and confusion; distance or melding	Blurred personal boundaries, sense of lostness
3–3	Confusion about which parental dyadic set of rules to follow	Exaggeration of in-and-out introspective behavior possible	Competition, lack of felt appreciation; threatened by possible marriage failure
4–4	Complementary roles, smoothing, may cut out family members	Overwhelming need to accommodate new family members into some kind of Gestalt associated with space, place, and pain in the family	Feelings of guilt and responsibility for pain in the family; need for approval of efforts

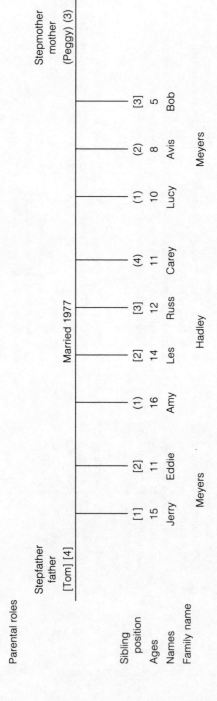

Figure 10–5 Step-family: The Meyers.

father and his brother, they remember the way he took care of their emotional needs; each time he leaves, they experience a sense of loss. It was difficult for Eddie to establish his place in this very complex step-family. At first, he preferred to come when most of the Hadley children were visiting their father. With the passage of time, coming and going has become easier and disputes and conflicts normal.

A year after they were married, Tom and Peggy began having children of their own. They added three more children to the family, creating very complex, blurred roles. Although Lucy is the first child of the new marriage, she is not a first to either parent. The family environment is too large and complex to shape many first-sibling patterns. She may have the blended pattern of a third child, for her father, and a fifth child, for her mother. Similarly, Avis and Bob may develop the characteristics of blended sibling positions. The patterns established for these blended roles are still unknown, but it may be assumed that each sibling has distinct jobs for serving the family system.

Comparisons of Family Forms

Comparisons of the structure, individual and family needs, and information processing in single-parent families and step-families provide means of exploring the effects of family environment on sibling positions.

Structure

The family structure provides information about the interaction of family members, boundaries, rules, and roles (see Table 10–4). Boundaries define the family and the people within the family as units separate from other systems and subsystems. Regulating the interactional processes of information, people, and objects, boundaries serve as perceptual filters that maintain a given family's form. Rules guide members within their specific roles so that the needs of the family and individuals are met within the boundaries of the family and family relationships. The structural patterns of dysfunctional families are exaggerations or deletions of the structural patterns of functional families.

Individual and Family Needs

A basic purpose of the family system is to facilitate the fulfillment of individual and family needs (see Table 10–5). The goals of individuals and family units determine the energy and direction of strategies to meet these needs. The goals tend to be inferential, because the needs often operate on an

Table 10–4 Structure in functional nuclear families, single-parent families, and step-families.

Variables	Functional nuclear family	Single-parent family	Step-family
Family members	Hierarchies clear, membership stable; relationships in family predictable	Hierarchies unclear; interrupted by loss of a member; structure unpredictable; new structure emerging	Loss of members, new members added; hierarchies unclear; relationships interrupted by missing members; structure changing and unpredictable; new structure emerging
Boundaries	Filters to screen out objectionable information, accept and process relevant information; established and adaptive	Blurring of parent-child boundaries because of loss of one parent; changes in sibling subsystem boundaries possible	Boundaries blurred and possibly functioning in confusing ways; rigid subsystem boundaries; difficulty of marital system in preserving its boundaries
Rules	Regulation of behaviors with predictability, whether implicit or explicit	Need to reestablish and adapt rules to new conditions and contexts	Rules unpredictable, implicit, confusing; at least 2 parental sets of rules plus those of all subsystems; roles of enforcers and reinforcers of rules possibly confused
Roles	Most needs met by the ascribed and assumed roles in the family	Some roles missing, particularly parental; productivity and stability roles affected	Some roles missing; some duplicated; needs met sporadically or not at all

Table 10–5 Individual and family needs in functional nuclear families, single-parent families, and step-families.

Needs	Functional nuclear family	Single-parent family	Step-family
Productivity	Met by individual and family efforts	Sporadic, gaps, and uncertainty	Sporadic, gaps, and uncertainty
Stability	Conditions mostly stable with instability related to growth and change	Unstable; roles, rules, and boundaries modified; imbalance created by loss of one set of values	Unstable; roles, rules, and boundaries forming, sometimes in conflict with different values
Sense of belonging	Family membership assured most of the time	Threatened because of loss of member(s); fear of losing parental support	Sometimes very unstable, with subgroups threatening and threatened; divided loyalties among parents and siblings
Intimacy	Levels and kinds established and dependable	Questionable quality, quantity, and motives	Questionable, may be stable in subgroups
Dependency	Developmental in nature, appropriate and predictable	Shifts toward more or less because of fear of rejection, loss, and abandonment	Unclear, other issues may take precedence; fear of rejection, loss, abandonment, and competition

implicit level. Inferred goals can be made explicit, however, by observing the roles that are active in the family system to accomplish the goals.

Information Processing

Families must adapt to changes in individuals and in the family system as family members learn new things, want and need different things from each other, and go through development stages. Not only crises, but also the steady flow of life makes demands on individuals and systems that require energy and attention from the family.

In a functional family, changes may be disruptive, but the family stabilizes fairly rapidly as the changes are integrated into the lifestyle of the family. Single-parent families and step-families often resist change, however, blocking adaptation to change because of the pain associated with disruptive change in the past. The fear of more changes may obstruct a realistic view of the nature of the change, whether it involves rules, roles, or intimacy needs.

Information processing is vital as the family fluctuates from stability to instability. Energy flow, information flow, and affect are variables that make it possible to compare the ways in which information processing maintains the family system (see Table 10–6). Energy flow, discernible in the actions and interactions of family members, reveals vital and stagnant areas. The amount of information, and the direction in which it passes between family members as well as in and out of family, are also evident in the energy flow. Family members interact to regulate energy, rules, and roles and to direct the flow of information in the family and the actions and reactions of the individuals and relationship units of the system. The affect of family members is one indication of their feelings toward themselves and other family members. It is part of the energy and information flow, as affect influences the family's ability to function productively. The ebb and flow of affect in a given family indicates whether the relationships within the family are nurturing.

Sibling Position Issues

When the Brown family lost their husband and father (see Figure 10–2), the response patterns of each family member interacted with the stages of grieving and with the family dynamics of a changed family structure, intense and different individual and family needs, and information processing. The major membership issue for the Brown family was the loss of one parent who had filled many roles, emotionally and instrumentally, for the family as a unit and for individuals in the family. Because his absence caused many changes in the family system, new rules had to be established, some of them formulated at the

Table 10–6 Information processing in functional nuclear families, single-parent families, and step-families.

Variables	Functional nuclear family	Single-parent family	Step-family
Energy flow	Predictable, open	Old patterns not always feasible, erratic and/or rigid at times; whimiscal	Patterns not established; erratic and/or rigid at times; whimiscal
Information flow	In and out of family and subsystems	Clear and abundant information needed, but may be lacking, confusing, or untrustworthy because of erratic energy flow	Clear and relevant information needed, but may be lacking or confusing because of erratic energy flow
Affect	Nurturing, predictable	Unpredictable; naturalness sometimes blocked by fear, anger, hurt, bitterness, suspicion, or guilt	Unpredictable; sexual issues between step-family members possible; naturalness sometimes blocked by fear, anger, hurt, bitterness, suspicion, or guilt

implicit level, to meet the emergency and survival needs of the family. Later, as the family stabilized, the rules were modified to conform to the normal development needs of the family.

When Dan died, Andrea no longer had an adult companion to share family responsibilities, love, decisions, and activities. The children missed their father and, consequently, wanted more from their mother than in the past. Sometimes, but not always, she could meet their needs. Furthermore, she needed more support and help from the children than she had in the past.

The modified structure of the family caused dramatic changes that made relationships unpredictable. Routines were interrupted and many of the tasks and services that had been taken for granted were not completed. The planning and the follow-through of those tasks and services that were completed took much energy, caused conflict, or were done in a sloppy fashion. For a while, standards of performance and values shifted, for some family members more than others. Andrea, for example, who had been a loving, but firm, taskmaster of family chores, became unpredictable in her expectations and in her supervision of the children. This was confusing both to her and to the children.

Because the roles, expectations, and rules in the family changed with the emotional turmoil, Andrea and the children exaggerated characteristic sibling response patterns. For example, to compensate for Andrea's lack of consistent supervision of family chores, Cynthia, the first sibling, was bossier than usual and demanded perfection in herself and the others. She was confused by her own behavior, especially her intolerance of her mother's performance. As the first child, Cynthia was responsible to her father for everyone in the family. His death did not change the assignment. Moreover, first children often assume that they must perform the roles abandoned by the missing parent. Cynthia's sense of responsibility was heightened, therefore, and she struggled to be an "adult" and meet the expectations of both her parents.

The love and concern that Cynthia felt for her mother, coupled with her job assignment, made her a willing confidant for her mother. At times, however, she was totally overwhelmed by her mother's pain, her own pain and confusion, and the needs of her two younger siblings. She reacted to this psychological threat by becoming hopeless at times. She longed for her father. Her mood and appearance were dark, and she seemed incapable of performing her jobs.

As the second child, Tom was expected to read the underlying structure, to help make the implicit information explicit, and to demonstrate the incongruencies between the implicit and explicit rules in the family. He was also primarily responsible for his mother. For a time, the combination of his mother's pain and his own, plus that of his brother and sister, was too much for Tom, and he became unavailable for expected chores and support. Occasionally, he responded to the unexpressed emotions and the confusion in the family by tattling more frequently on his older sister and younger brother. It was his attempt to flush out the incongruency between implicit expectations and explicit behavior. Tom needed reassurance that his place in the family was secure. In a family without an adult male role model, he needed recognition of his worth as a prized family member, without the impossible burden of being "the man" of the house.

One moment Chris would cling to anyone who would allow it, the next moment he would be gone into the neighborhood, playing with friends as if nothing had happened. As the third child, he was responsible for the quality of the marital relationship. Losing his father was an emotional blow to him, but he also lost the reality of the marital relationship. In one sense, his job was eradicated; in another sense, he still had to interpret and monitor relationships in the family based on the marital relationship, but had to apply the rules of the marriage as they were before his father's death. Relationships within the family were different because of the changed structure and adjustments that were being made. All these factors increased his uncertainties, fostering a sense of having no choices for balancing and fixing relationships in the family. Mixed with grief for his father, Chris experienced anger because he had no choice about losing his father.

The levels and kinds of intimacy in the family were changed by Dan's unexpected death. These changes threatened the sense of belonging in all family members. Each sibling reacted to this threat in a way that was typical of his or her sibling position. For example, Chris would go into his room and stay by himself for hours until someone went after him and either stayed with him or brought him out to the family. This pattern was an exaggeration of patterns he had followed when he was upset and his father was alive. When he withdrew from the family, Chris knew that eventually his father or mother would find him or send someone to find him.

The quality of the relationship that the children had experienced with their father also affected their responses. All the children had loved their father and had received encouragement, discipline, and physical affection from him. Cynthia had relied on her father for direction and specific information. Now that he was gone, she needed more than the usual assurance that she was carrying out her assignment satisfactorily. Tom lost his place in the family temporarily, because the membership structure shifted. With the grieving and emotional turmoil in the family, he did not know where he belonged. He needed implicit and explicit affirmation about his place and importance in the family. Chris responded to all the shifts in relationships in the family by moving in and out of relationships, clinging one moment and leaving the next.

Hierarchical boundaries in the family structure changed as Andrea struggled for stability and security. The normal shifting of parental roles to older siblings was intensified, as Andrea felt the need to confide in someone and share her burdens. As a fourth child herself, Andrea had always worked for family intimacy and unity. She stressed doing things together and doing things for each other. Dan had provided the balance for family members' legitimate separate activities. With her husband gone, Andrea's responsibility for keeping the family together was huge and frightening. She clung to the children, insisting that they do many more things together, perhaps unconsciously guarding against another loss.

The characteristic tendency of fourth children to take the blame for anything wrong in the family system was compounded by Andrea's guilt that she was alive and her husband was dead. Any conflict among the children or between her and the children assumed exaggerated importance to her. Things that she had handled easily in the past were often unmanageable now. When overwhelmed by family chaos and disharmony, fourth children compensate by cutting down the size of the arena; thus, Andrea ignored things or, really, no longer saw them as relevant to her.

When Andrea used the insurance money for training and later took a full-time job, she shifted more responsibility for the home to the children, especially to Cynthia. These responsibilities moved Cynthia out of the sibling subsystem and into the parent subsystem. Tom received some of this responsibility, too, as he was designated the "man of the family." Andrea enlisted his aid in solving problems or doing things that in the past would have been done by his father. These shifts were emergency survival strategies.

As the family moved through the grieving stages with appropriate adjustments and compensations, hierarchical boundaries shifted again, leaving Andrea the only one in the parent subsystem. As Andrea gained confidence in her own abilities, she adjusted to living as a single parent. She shared some of her adult needs and confidences with extended family members and friends. She also encouraged her children to be active in their own interests.

REFERENCES

Ahrons, C. (1981). The binuclear family: Two step-families, two houses. *Step-Family Bulletin,* *1*(2), 5–6.

Glenwick, D. S., & Mowerey, J. D. (1986). When parents become peers: Loss of intergenerational boundaries in single-parent families. *Family Relations, 35,* 57–62.

Mills, D. (1984). A model for step-family development. *Family Relations, 33,* 365–372.

Schulman, G. D. (1972). Myths that intrude on the adaptation of the step-family. *Social Casework,* *49,* 131–139.

CHAPTER 11

Parenting Issues for Nuclear Families, Single-Parent Families, and Step-Families

The family of origin is the training ground for parenthood. In the family, children learn and practice how to get along with others, how to influence others, how to love and nurture others, and generally how to interact with others. Thus, many factors in the family of origin affect the kind of parent that a person will be. One of these factors is the individual's sibling position.

As each parent brings his or her unique training to parenthood, the sibling position of each influences their joint efforts to raise their children. Therefore, the sibling position interaction in the mother-father-child triangle is as influential in parenting as it is in the interaction in the parent-child dyad. This is true not only in the traditional nuclear family, but also in the single-parent family and the step-family. Even though dead or absent from everyday physical interaction, a missing parent continues to be influential through symbolic interactions in the minds of the remaining family members. In the case of divorce, children are frequently involved with both parents so that some kind of interaction in the triangle is perpetuated.

Guidelines for Parenting First Children

Make parental expectations explicit and reachable. Because first children worry about gaining approval and being "good enough," parents need to be explicit about their expectations and to set standards that first children can reach. These expectations should be defined firmly, but not harshly. Children in all sibling positions benefit when parental expectations are clear and reachable, but this is especially important for first children.

Reassure first children whenever possible that they are "on target." First children thrive when praise is explicit and when the implicit messages indicate approval of their activities. This kind of feedback boosts their self-esteem; however, the impact on their self-esteem is fleeting. It is helpful also to remind first children of past accomplishments.

Recognize the intent of first children to be on target even when their action is not appropriate. When first children learn that they have made a mistake, they often fail to hear the rest of the message. Parents should first validate the intent of first children by recognizing what they were trying to do and then point out that their approach did not get the results intended. It is quite enlightening at times to listen to first children explain their behavior. For example, one first child confronted a teacher in a very belligerent manner. His parents and others told him not to talk that way to teachers, but the child remained "stony" and "immovable." He explained that he thought the teacher's actions were unfair, and he was trying to right what he saw as a wrong. By recognizing his intent to do right, his parents were able to make him understand that the way in which he was trying to "right" the injustice was inappropriate.

Tell first children that they are also appreciated for who they are. First children sometimes feel that others appreciate them only for what they can produce. By telling them that they are appreciated for themselves, parents validate their "centralness." It also teaches them that they are sufficient, regardless of what they do or do not produce.

Give first children a great deal of information by providing logical explanations for what they are required to do. In other words, use inductive reasoning. First children make sense of their world by logical analysis of explicit details. They understand discipline in the same way. Therefore, explanations help first children, and when they respond with questions, it helps to give the explanation again. The information should be given in a nonpunishing way, however. If the parent's tone of voice is harsh, angry, and loud, first children hear only the disapproval, not the content of the message. Then, they are immediately ready to fight for the rightness of their position.

Help first children to know that they have done enough. First children continue to search for information long after it is necessary. A parental reminder that they have done enough encourages them to limit their obsessive, compulsive behavior. Too often, first children receive the opposite message from parents. One first child commented that her mother did not notice that she had received five solid A's for the term, but rather focused immediately on the one mark that was an A-. (Her mother was a first child.)

Be affectionate. First children like to appear to others as strong, unemotional types. Their defensive stances sometimes make them seem aloof. Even though they may not admit it, however, first children have as much need as anyone to be touched and told that they are loved.

Validate the feelings of first children, and help them learn about emotion by connecting it to their cognitive processes. First children need to understand the reasons for their feelings so that their feelings make sense to them. Parents can help by pushing first children to connect their feelings to events, as well as to what they think about those events.

Emphasize enjoying the process as much as or more than the results. First children focus on results because of their role in the family. It is important to remind them to have fun and enjoy what they are doing. Otherwise, they can become so involved in finishing the task that they forget to enjoy the path to their goal.

Remember that first children act out the unresolved issues of the parent whose primary function is productivity, usually the father in traditional families. When first children are misbehaving in some way, fathers should examine their own emotional process for unresolved issues. Many times, first children are simply acting out the unfulfilled fantasies, dreams, or unresolved emotional issues of their father. This is related to an intergenerational transmission. One father, Warren, grew up in a family where his own father, John, was extremely angry with his mother—Warren's grandmother. John had not learned to deal openly with his anger toward his mother, however, and often vented his anger on his wife. Warren felt a great deal of anger toward his wife as well, but it did not make any logical sense to him; his wife's behavior did not merit the intensity of the anger he felt. Consequently, he felt inhibited in expressing the anger. Warren's daughter, a first sibling, constantly argued with her mother and exhibited tremendous emotion toward her. Therapy revealed that the daughter was simply acting out the unresolved anger of husbands toward wives through generations of their family.

Guidelines for Parenting Second Children

Make parental expectations explicit to reduce incongruencies and to facilitate the acknowledgment of messages and emotions. Second children need parents to be explicit about their expectations in order to reduce the discrepancies between the implicit underlying structure and the explicit messages. Parents should also be explicit about their own feelings, nonverbal messages, and attitudes. Second children sense these intuitively, and they are less confused when parents acknowledge their own responsibility for their feelings.

Be affectionate. Parents' demonstration of affection helps second children feel that they have a place. Affection alone is not sufficient to establish a "sense of place" for second children, but it is certainly a contributing factor. Parents should also assist second children in establishing boundaries by letting them know that it is all right to refuse affection if they wish, as long as they do not refuse it all the time. Parents can help second children understand how much affection is appropriate, in what contexts it should be expressed, and how to initiate and receive it without violating another person's boundaries.

Reassure second children that they will always have a "place." Second children need both a physical place and a psychological place in order to feel secure. Although second children may have to share a room with other siblings, parents should make sure that second children have a place somewhere in the house that is theirs (e.g., a desk or a chair of their own). Parents can provide an emotional place for second children by reminding them that even when they are not physically present and even when they are adults, they will always have a place in the family and with their parents.

Be clearly available and supportive, but not involved in the emotion of second children. When second children are upset or crying, parents should be available to them and should reassure them that they still have an important place in the family and with their parents. Sometimes, discipline threatens the sense of place of second children. When this happens, they may become angry—screaming, throwing tantrums, and behaving hysterically. It is important for parents to remain available, but uninvolved with the emotions.

When second children are polarized, respond from the opposite pole. When second children are polarized affectively, parents should not focus explicitly on their affect, but rather should try to move them away from it by making statements such as "Later, when you have calmed down, we can talk about it" and holding them. Thus, when second children are highly emotional, parents should be rational so that they can help the children to sort through what is happening to them. If parents are upset and involved in their children's pain, second children sense it and add the parents' pain to their own. This increases the polarization. When second children are polarized cognitively, parents should try to help them make their underlying affect explicit. Asking questions such as "What are you feeling?" helps second children integrate the middle parts between the two poles.

Help second children separate their emotions from the emotions of those around them. Questions such as "Is this what you are feeling, or is this what someone else is feeling?" help second children step outside the situation to reach a cognitive understanding of the melding process that allows them to release the emotions that are not theirs. Of course, it also helps when parents are explicit about their own feelings and openly accept responsibility for their own feelings, thus relieving the children of this responsibility.

When second children assume that they have said something, but they have not, simply ask them if there is something that they have forgotten to mention. Parental condemnation for the failure of second children to make something explicit—when they believe that they have done so—solves no problem. Rather, it leads to arguments. It is better simply to ask as a matter of interest if they have forgotten to say something. When parents have the attitude of wanting to know more information, second children are freer to examine what their parents need to know.

Do not offer long explanations: instead, ask second children what they do not understand and fill in the missing pieces. Additional explanation is often confusing to second children. As a rule of thumb, parents should first ask second children what they do not understand, then describe and explain the parts that are missing.

In trying to understand the experience of second children, explore their visual imagery and use visual metaphors to help them understand. Second children often process experience in highly visual ways, such as internal "movies" and "pictures." If parents ask them to describe these visual images, parents have a better understanding of the cognitive and affective experience of their second children. In conversations with second children, it is useful to use visual metaphors in addition to logical explanation.

Remember that second children act out the unresolved issues of the parent whose primary function is stability, usually the mother in traditional families. One second child described her mother's unresolved family issues in the following way:

> My mother was very rebellious with her own parents, mostly because she was always saddled with the responsibilities that should have been my grandmother's . . . things like taking care of the home and baby sister.

This daughter was in therapy because her strong feelings against getting married, having children, or cleaning anybody's house confused her. When second children have problems, parents should examine the mother's emotional tension for possible connections.

Guidelines for Parenting Third Children

Be explicit about expectations and rules for interactions. Parents can help third children by clearly stating their expectations for interaction and by explicitly negotiating the rules for parent-child interactions, such as not interrupting, listening attentively to each other, and adopting a positive attitude. This helps the child understand the underlying principles of the relationship.

Be affectionate. Third children like affection, but they are not always good at initiating it. Therefore, it is important for parents to take the initiative and to respond affectionately to any initiative of third children. This helps third children feel a connection with parents and meets their need for inclusion in family relationships.

Assist third children in generating and maintaining choices. Because third children like to have choices available, they respond favorably when parents explore alternatives with them. Although it is important for parents to offer choices to children in any sibling position, it is crucial for third children. Without choices, third children feel trapped and limited. Sometimes, like any other child, third children are rash in the choices they make; therefore, parents should point out the consequences attached to specific choices.

Do not take choices away from third children by cornering them or forcing them to choose. Third children become stubborn and angry when others try to force them to make a choice. If they can, they withdraw from the situation; if they cannot withdraw, they fight to keep choices available. Additional pressure at this point only escalates the stubborn, resistive behavior. Parents should explore alternatives and give third children time to make a choice.

Allow third children to be in and out. It is impossible to force third children to interact when they need to go away. Even if they remain physically present, they can leave psychologically. By pushing the issue, parents simply raise the defenses of third children. Third children need time to study and work out problems in their own mind; then they will return to the relationship.

Assure third children of their parents' availability when they return. Parents build trust with third children by saying something like "You probably need to think about it on your own; I'll be here when you are ready to talk about it." When such messages are clear, third children learn that their parents care about them whether they are in or out. If parents interpret the going away as stubbornness, contrariness, or abandonment and respond in kind, third children may be confused and hurt. Such experiences suggest to them that their parents cannot be trusted.

Recognize that even when third children are on the "periphery," they are still involved and care. Because of their in-and-out behavior, third children sometimes appear to be uninvolved in family discussions or events. Yet, parents are often amazed at the amount and kind of information that third children have absorbed. Perhaps parents should remind themselves that third children are involved and care, although it may not appear so. Sometimes, all that third children need is for someone to include them by making a connection to them.

Help third children make connections by exploring with them the underlying principles of how things work. Third children like to know how to get from point to point, but they also want to learn to generalize the principle used so that they can apply it in a similar context. The explanations of parents, teachers, and therapists often lack these kinds of connections, however. Parents should take time to explore connections with third children by asking questions such as "What puzzles you about that?" "Do you see any connection between these two events?" The responses of third children to such inquiries are often very enlightening.

When establishing rules for behavior, help third children see the connection between the rule and the smooth function of the family. When third children understand that a rule helps balance family relationships, they are more likely to abide by the rule. It is helpful to explore alternate ways of complying with the rules so that third children focus on the principle behind the rule rather than what they perceive as the rigid behavior associated with it. Parents can keep third children from focusing on the freedom lost as a result of the rule by emphasizing what specific rules allow third children to do rather than what they prevent third children from doing.

Remember that third children act out the unresolved marital issues and pain in the marriage. When parents acknowledge their part in the problems of the marital relationship and are working toward resolution, third children do not usually have behavior problems. When parents try to cover up chronic tension and pain in the marriage, however, third children can become depressed, isolated, delinquent, or aggressive. Parents need to realize that although the quality of their marriage affects all their children, it has a particular impact on third children. Thus, when third children are having difficulty, parents should examine their marriage, be explicit about any marital tension, and work toward resolution. Third children need to know that their parents acknowledge the tension and do not expect the third children to manage it.

Guidelines for Parenting Fourth Children

Be explicit about expectations and feelings in the family. When parents are explicit about their expectations for all their children, the children in the other sibling positions usually do their part, facilitating movement toward the family task or purpose. Thus, it becomes easier for fourth children to ensure harmony and unity in the family. A focus on expectations and feelings related to specific tasks helps fourth children limit the size of their job.

Be affectionate. Parents' expression of affection toward them not only helps fourth children feel love and appreciation, but also adds to the feelings of unity and harmony in the family. Expressions of the love that parents have for each of their children make them feel even more secure. Affection smooths over disruptions so that the family can continue to move toward its purposes and goals. Because they are usually the ones who initiate affectionate behaviors in the family, fourth children respond very positively when parents show affection.

Acknowledge responsibility for personal feelings and contributions to disruptions. By acknowledging their feelings and accepting at least part of the responsibility for conflict and other disruptions in the family, parents help fourth children to feel less responsible for family tension. Fourth children learn that other people recognize their own contribution to tension and can resolve it. Such a discovery is usually a relief to fourth children.

Do not justify actions as a parent. Parents do not need to give fourth children reasons for their behavior as parents, as fourth children may perceive such justifications as additional burdens. Rather parents should explain how the rule or behavior fits some overall purpose for the family. This helps fourth children to see the way in which the parts fit into the whole.

Reassure fourth children that they are not responsible for other people's feelings. Because fourth children tend to be the "garbage collectors" of other people's emotions, they often feel that they are at fault in some mystical way for what others are feeling. By reassuring fourth children that they are not to blame for all the tension, disruption, and emotion that other family members carry, parents help them disengage from the "garbage."

When fourth children overdramatize, ignore it at times and confront them about it at other times. Fourth children tend to overdo emotional reactions. "I am just going to die!" or "Everything is falling apart!" are common responses of fourth children to minor events. The intensity of observable behavior connected to the event that elicits these responses and the statements that fourth children make simply do not match. Sometimes, parents should ignore the over-dramatizations. At other times, parents can say things such as "Oh, come on now, it is not nearly that bad " or "Let me know when you are finished with the dramatics." Such statements cause fourth children to look at their dramatic behavior through someone else's eyes.

When fourth children are impulsive, set boundaries and limits. Parents can help fourth children limit their impulsive behavior by pointing out that such behavior sometimes disrupts the harmony of the family as a whole. Parents should not attempt to rid fourth children of their spontaneity, but rather to teach them when it is appropriate and when it is not.

Teach fourth children that they can assert their own opinions, feelings, and requests without being aggressive or breaking rules. Fourth children often fail to state their own preferences or feelings in order to placate others and bring unity to the family. They sometimes lose sight of the fact that they also have individual needs and preferences to which other family members should respond.

Help fourth children break the whole into parts. Sometimes, fourth children seem uncooperative or resist parental requests because "something" seems overwhelming to them. Parents can help them by breaking down large tasks into more specific steps and by helping fourth children see the relationship of the whole to its parts. When this happens, fourth children tend to be more productive.

Remember that fourth children act out the family tension and pain. Fourth children can be overwhelmed by pain, sadness, grief, or chaos that originates anywhere in the family system, either in individuals or in relationships. Therefore, when fourth children have behavior problems, the family should investigate to determine who or what relationships are suffering. Parents can explore with fourth children what they sense is happening in the family and who is experiencing pain. This makes it possible to send help where it resolves the behavior problems of the fourth children.

Impact of Sibling Positions on Parenting

As mentioned earlier, the way in which parents carry out their parenting role is influenced by their sibling positions. First siblings are likely to have high expectations for all their children, because they emphasize productivity and results. They are also likely to rely on rational, logical, and wordy explanations to motivate and discipline their children, rather than on underlying emotions and feelings. Because of their need to be right, first sibling parents have difficulty being and appearing nondefensive to their children. As a result, they often find themselves in a power struggle with each of their children, but especially with the first. When first sibling parents push for decisions and results, they may receive cooperation from first and fourth children, take choices away from third children, and cause second children to adopt a stubborn stance.

Second sibling parents have difficulty making all their expectations explicit. They often assume that they have been clear when they have not been at all clear. When second sibling parents are polarized affectively, they appear irrational to their children. First children may resist the affect, second children are immobilized by the affect, third children may go away, and fourth children feel responsible for the situation. Some children, particularly first children, feel that their privacy has been invaded if their second sibling parents push them too much to acknowledge their implicit feelings and attitudes. Second sibling parents also have a tendency to meld with the pain, sadness, and hurt that their children often feel as a natural part of their life experience. This melding neutralizes their power as decisive and helpful parents.

Third sibling parents are likely to be involved with their children as part of a triangle. Not only do they have their own unique relationship with each child, but also they are involved with their spouse about each child. In fact, both third and fourth sibling parents tend to monitor family connections and make sure that their spouses are involved with the children. In contrast, first siblings make connections with their children individually and fail to mention it to their spouses.

The challenge for parents who are third siblings is to be available when their children need them. Because of their in-and-out behavior in relationships, third sibling parents can at times seem uninvolved and uncaring to their children. If their spouse is not actively involved in the parenting, third sibling parents may begin to feel trapped, fearing that they have no choices. Third sibling parents need freedom to share the responsibility of parenting and freedom to do other things besides parenting.

Fourth sibling parents can be overwhelmed by the Gestalt of parenting. When their children are trying to cope with the normal developmental tasks and problems of growing up, fourth sibling parents may feel guilty because they are not doing more to protect their children from suffering. When their spouse is not involved in the parenting, fourth sibling parents feel angry and resentful. Parents who are fourth siblings usually urge the rest of the family to participate in activities that develop family harmony and unity. As it is the duty of fourth sibling parents to emphasize family togetherness, they feel threatened if family members seem to prefer to go their own way.

Effects of Sibling Positions on Parent-Child Interaction

The following example illustrates the usefulness of sibling position information in understanding the interaction between parents and children. Suzanne and David had been married for 18 years and had four children. Suzanne was the first child in her family; David, the third child in his. Mike, their oldest child, was 14.

Mike had been a good student all through grade school. As he entered junior high school, however, his grades began to fall. Instead of As, he began to receive some Bs and Cs. Being a first child, Suzanne was overly concerned about her son's diminished productivity and constantly reminded him about homework as soon as he came home from school. She started asking many questions about whether Mike had finished his work in each class, whether the teacher had returned any assignments, and whether he was making progress on specific projects. His answers to her questions were somewhat vague at times and purposely evasive at other times.

Mike told the therapist that his mother intruded in his life constantly, asking questions, demanding answers, and wanting to know everything. From Suzanne's point of view, her questions were simply an attempt to obtain more information, and the fact that Mike would not give it to her was highly upsetting. Her anxiety and frustration led to more questioning and more exaggerated behavior which, of course, made Mike even more stony and immovable. As Suzanne pushed harder and harder, the conflict intensified until they were both shouting. The underlying issue was who was most right. Suzanne felt that she was failing as a parent. Mike also felt that he was failing in that he was unable to obtain support and approval from either parent. Of course, neither admitted these feelings to the other.

David, the father, performed his role as a third child very well. He was in the middle of the relationship between Suzanne and Mike, trying to balance the conflict. At times, David would talk to Suzanne about the way that she constantly nagged Mike about his schoolwork, but she perceived this as a criticism of her parenting and resented it very much. Although not an explicit part of the dynamics in this case, the adequacy of her performance was an issue for Suzanne, and she was not receiving approval from either her husband or her son. She would get angry, she and David would fight, and David would go to his study and read a book.

After these fights, it was often several days before David was as close and responsive to Suzanne as he usually was. During this time, Mike kept to himself a great deal and seemed very moody when anyone else tried to reach out to him. Mike complained regularly that his mother was unfair, but he admitted in therapy that he was most distressed by his sense of responsibility for the fights that his parents were having. As David had retreated to his study to work out the issues (a third-child strategy), Mike had become more and more isolated from everyone (a first child tendency to act on the father's unresolved emotional issues). The tension between Suzanne and Mike became so bad that at the slightest edge in Suzanne's voice, Mike became immovable, lashing out with highly verbal, logical defenses to justify his refusal to give her information.

Clearly, the recognized tendencies of first-sibling parents and third-sibling parents can be used to understand some of the underlying sibling position issues of this parenting triangle. As a first sibling parent, for example, Suzanne tended to ask too many questions, expected too much of Mike, and sent messages to him that his performance was unsatisfactory. This, of course, threatened Mike's sense of well-being. The issue of who was most right escalated into a full-scale battle that always ended with both mother and son threatened and neither willing to move to accommodate the other.

David always entered the fray as a mediator. It was his job in his family of origin to balance dyadic relationships, and he continued to do this as a father. When the pain became too great, he retreated psychologically to sort out the issues. By the time he returned, Suzanne had already decided that his going away was an indication of his disapproval of her, and she was not psychologically available to him.

Any parent-child interaction can be explored by examining the characteristic response patterns of both the parent's sibling position and the child's sibling position, and using the information obtained to complement other knowledge.

Loyalty Issues

In single-parent families and step-families, parent-child interaction is affected by loyalties to absent parents. First children are loyal to parental expectations, especially those of their father. If he is not living with the family, first children think that they must assume his responsibilities. This assumption usually results in being overly responsible for their siblings and their mother, with skewed hierarchical boundaries as the result. With their father absent, first children base their interpretation of his expectations on earlier interactions with him and current contacts with him, if he is living, as well as on interactions with their mother. If their father is dead or has no contact with them, first children extrapolate expectations from stories about their father. Any discrepancies between the expectations of their father and the expectations of their mother, sometimes including those of their stepfather, as first children perceive them, result in constant friction. The source of conflict is often at an implicit level, however.

A focus on past rules is almost always evident in single-parent families and step-families. Knowingly or unknowingly, first children sabotage new rules when a parent is missing or when one is added. They may make statements to siblings or a parent, sometimes quietly, indicating the wrongness of a situation: "But, Mom, that is not the way we do things!" All the incongruencies between new implicit rules and the explicit rules followed in the past affect second children, because they assimilate the tension that is created.

For second children, loyalty issues are usually connected to their mother. They may be melded with their mother's wishes and emotional state even if they do not live with her. On the other hand, they may move away from their mother's, their own, and other family member's pain. Because most loyalty issues are implicit, second children sense the confusion and pain, absorb it, and are burdened by it. They may act it out in stubborn, stupid behavior; they may polarize cognitively as a way of ignoring it; they may refuse to be involved with the family; or they may act helpless and lost. This behavior is very confusing to single parents, parents, and step-parents who may be involved.

Because third siblings are responsible for the marital relationship, the absence or death of a parent is a personal failure to them. In single-parent families, third children continue to support the rules and values of the past marital relationship and usually have the family's approval to do so. In step-families, however, loyalty to the absent parent is confounded by the need to support a new marital relationship and to help the remaining parent to be happy. This situation can be very confusing to third children.

Although fourth children may be devastated by the loss of a parent, their loyalty is to the fantasy of the unity and harmony in the family before the loss. On one level, fourth children welcome a new marriage and an opportunity to recreate the wholeness of the past family. On another level, they sense the pain of the "ghost" in their midst and assume responsibility for everyone's pain. If the absent parent is living in another household, fourth children may return from a visit with dramatic descriptions, such as "You should see my dad! He is soooooooooo happy!"

Interactions in Single-Parent Families

The single-parent family presents some unique considerations in an examination of the impact of sibling positions on parent-child interactions. Regardless of the way in which the parent became single, the roles in the family that relate to productivity and stability change. Children and parents have been traumatized by the loss of a spouse and parent, and their need for support from other people increases several-fold.

Often, single parents must spend a great deal of their time and energy in earning a living, which means that children usually have to assume additional responsibilities for taking care of themselves, housekeeping, cooking, and sometimes even meeting financial needs. Although tired when they return home from work, single parents must face the demands of children and other duties related to the household. As a result, the family's stability needs increase. As all families, the needs for productivity and stability are interwoven. However, for single-parent families, the awareness that "we" need to be productive to remain stable and "we" need to be stable to become productive is heightened because only one parent is available to meet these needs.

The family's need for increased productivity and stability leads to exaggerations of many of the characteristic sibling response patterns. For example, first and second children, regardless of gender, may assume the roles of parents and rule enforcers when a parent is absent. If the father is absent, the first child often begins to act as a surrogate father to the rest of the children. When either the first or second sibling assumes the role of surrogate parent, the resulting blurred hierarchical boundaries usually produce conflict in his or her relationship with the other siblings. The child parents the other children with the encouragement of his or her parent, but the single parent sometimes responds to the surrogate as a child. This is very confusing to everyone, but especially to the child expected to live in two worlds.

Third and fourth children are a vital part of these dynamics as they fight with first and second children about their bossiness as surrogate parents. Because of the shifting rules for relationships, third children are very confused. They may become super-bossy themselves, especially to younger siblings. Fourth children sense the tension in the family and push for equal treatment for everyone, while at the same time fighting with the third sibling. Single parents must clarify the hierarchy in the family and be explicit about rules and boundaries.

First children may act as a surrogate spouse to their mother in their father's absence. When the mother is the absent parent, second children may act as a surrogate spouse to their father. First children may also assume this role. It is not necessarily the intent of the parent or the child for this surrogate spouse type of role to develop. Rather, it is a function of the fact that first children feel responsible to each parent, and a single parent does not always have very many adult support systems.

Some incest patterns develop from the blurring of hierarchical boundaries and the adaptations of children to meet the needs of their parents. Although the children may be victims, at some level they accept incestuous behavior as part of their job assignment. Sorting through incest patterns with parents and children from the sibling position perspective may help them separate and function in more healthy ways.

In a single-parent family created by divorce, the parents often have a great deal of anger toward each other. First children who live with a mother who is very angry often fight their father's battle with their mother. Though they may not agree with or approve of their father they may continue to represent his position on matters in family discussions.

The following case, which involves a single-parent family, illustrates the impact of each family member's sibling position on the issues around divorce. Jamie, a second sibling, and Don, a first sibling, had been married 15 years when Don moved into his own apartment. Don and Jamie had four children: Margaret, 12; Sara, 9; John, 5; and Jim, 1. Jamie had become more and more distant in the marriage, and fights were constant. Don felt that he had done everything possible to please Jamie, but that nothing he did was ever good enough to suit her. Jamie's response to the separation was to become even more distant and isolated from her family and neighborhood. Over the next year, Don moved back into the house several times. Each attempt at reconciliation failed, however, and Don decided to get a divorce.

Jamie was bitter toward Don, but he continued to be involved with each of the children. Approximately two months after the divorce was finalized, the oldest daughter, Margaret, began to have behavior problems. She skipped school, wore excessive amounts of makeup and provocative clothes, smoked marijuana, and resisted everything her mother wanted her to do. Margaret continued to help parent the younger children, however, particularly when her younger sister, Sara, helped.

In therapy, Jamie began to see that Margaret had symbolically replaced Don and that she was continuing her parents' marital fights in the parent-child relationship. Margaret was angry with her mother because she felt that her mother had not given her father a chance (first child's support of the father's issue).

Interactions in Step-Families

The interactions of parents and children in step-families may become extremely complex, not only because of the numbers of systems, subsystems, and individuals involved, but also because of blurred, duplicated, and missing sibling and parental roles. Moreover, loyalty issues may become more complex and emphatic. The Williams family clearly demonstrates the ways in which sibling positions affect loyalty issues in parent-child interactions in step-families (see Figure 10-4).

When Jon and Barbara married, they each brought children from previous marriages to the family. Jon's former wife, Karen (a second sibling), divorced Jon and left the three children with him when Kelly was 7 and the twins, Susan and Beth were 3. She told Jon that she was unable to care for three children. After the divorce, she had minimal contact with the children. She called once in a while and, if she were in town, she might visit and bring gifts. Her life style was very different from that of the Williams family.

Barbara's two children, Sam and Lonnie, were older than Jon's children. When Barbara was asked about her former husband, Dave (a fourth sibling), she said that he was still one of the nicest guys in town, kind, loving to the children, but that he had about as much spine as a wet dishrag and was totally undependable. He called or visited Sam and Lonnie at least once a week and wanted to have them with him every other weekend. This arrangement did not always work out, however, because Sam and Lonnie were adolescents who had their own friends and weekend activities. They were also angry with their father. He had not remarried, but he told them every time he visited them that he was thinking about marrying, each time to a different woman. Yet, in the same breath he would tell them that, if he had his way, he would still be married to their mother. In this way, he constantly reminded his children of family ties and pointed out that he was still loyal to their mother, even though she was not loyal to him.

The marriage between Jon and Barbara was and continues to be a good marriage. Jon, a second sibling, tended to be very productive. He was also tender, empathic, and sensitive to Barbara's needs. Jon liked Barbara's wit, willingness to be involved, determination, and spunk. They had an excellent sexual relationship. They were affectionate in front of the children, and it was very obvious that they loved each other.

Sam had mixed feelings about his step-father, although he realized that Jon was everything that Dave, his biological father, was not. Sam knew that he could not count on Dave. In one incident, Jon got tickets for a football game and invited Sam to go with him. Sam really wanted to go, but he was torn by his feelings of loyalty to Dave. Sam finally called Dave to get permission to go. His dad said, "I don't know why you are asking me because I can't make those decisions for you." Then he paused and said, "That sure is a good idea. I wish that I had thought of that." Dave not only would not reassure his son by telling him that it was "Okay" to go with Jon, but he also implied that Sam should be going with him, Dave.

When Barbara heard about the conversation from Lonnie, her second child, she was furious. She told Sam that he should go with Jon whether Dave approved or not. He could do what his father wanted when he was with his father, but he should show a little consideration for others when he was in their family. Sam felt that he had to support his father and had a battle with his mother about whether Dave could ever be responsible. Sam did not go to the ball game as much as he wanted to see it.

As a third sibling, Barbara retreated into introspection to examine her feelings and the issues between her and her son. This made her emotionally unavailable to Jon, her husband. He had many feelings about what had happened, but he could not sort them out and make them explicit because neither Barbara nor Sam would talk to him.

Lonnie fought with Barbara, because she did not want to be a baby-sitter for her younger step-sisters. She did not fight with Jon, because he did not impose baby-sitting on her. He was willing to pay her for it. Barbara said that she was opposed to paying Lonnie because they were a family and needed to start behaving like a family. Kelly, the first child from Jon's first marriage, did not want to be "tended" by either Sam or Lonnie. Kelly had lived with her father in a single-parent family for a year and a half before he married Barbara. Although they sometimes had baby-sitters, Kelly had been given a great deal of responsibility. She said, "I can be just as responsible as Sam or Lonnie. I can take care of myself and the other kids." Barbara listened to her, but dismissed her ability. Jon said, "I do not understand Kelly. She has never been sullen and disobedient like she is over this baby-sitting issue." While trying to instill loyalty to the new family in her daughter, Barbara had not recognized Lonnie's need to maintain her place with her father by not becoming too involved with the new family. Kelly's desire to be recognized as the first child in her father's family and to receive approval for what she could do was also part of the issue in this triangle.

Susan and Beth, the twins, were happy to have so many people around. They clung to Jon, Barbara, and Kelly and wanted a great deal of affection and attention. They wanted the same from Sam and Lonnie, which Sam did not like. When Barbara was upset about the ball game incident, both Susan and Beth cried frequently and were whiny. The difference between the twins' behavior with their step-siblings and step-mother and Kelly's behavior was really puzzling to Jon. The twins seemed much happier, ate better, and played better, whereas Kelly was just the opposite.

Looking at this family from the perspective of sibling positions, it is clear that Kelly felt threatened because Sam, being older, seemed to be more central than she was. Furthermore, he and Lonnie had taken over many of the jobs that had helped her to feel productive and important before her father remarried. Being a second child, Lonnie fought with her mother so that Barbara would be involved with her and available to her, even though she knew implicitly that her mother always returned.

Therapy Applications for Individual, Couple, and Family Therapy

The interaction of the numerous client, therapist, environment, and therapy process variables is extremely complex. Explorations of the impact of sibling positions may provide unique information in therapy with individuals, couples, families of various forms, groups, and multigenerational families. As such, sibling positions become one more source of knowledge for therapists and their clients. The characteristic response patterns for sibling positions may be used to clarify the diagnoses and to develop treatment strategies.

CHAPTER *12*

Application of Sibling Position Concepts in Therapy

Although therapists can broaden their understanding of clients through a consideration of sibling positions it is important to remember that some of this information is not readily accessible to either therapists or clients. Because people are not usually focused on their behavior from the point of view of sibling positions, they are not aware of their sibling position response patterns. Moreover, many sibling position response patterns interact on an implicit level and are attached to assignments given at an implicit level. Therefore, the therapeutic setting provides an opportunity for therapists to learn about clients' sibling response patterns and their contribution to dysfunctional patterns. A family genogram, family sculpting, and various methods of family history taking are also very revealing. All therapeutic strategies and processes in therapy sessions may provide helpful sibling position information.

The Therapist

The sibling position response patterns of therapists themselves are a functional part of the process of therapy. Therapists' sibling positions influence their strategies for gathering information about their clients; their conceptualizations of the individual, couple, and family systems; and their expectations for clients. These sibling patterns interact with their formal training to form a unique style of therapy.

Therapists' sibling position patterns can be both helpful and detrimental in therapy. For example, therapists of the same sibling position as their clients have information and experiences that help them understand the client's perceptions, psychological defenses, family roles, and identity issues. Furthermore, they have information about the interaction of a person in that sibling position with others. Because sibling positions are always complementary to other sibling positions, therapists also have information about sibling positions other than their own. Finally, knowing something about the client from the sibling position perspective may help the therapist join the family more rapidly.

Therapists' sibling response patterns can be detrimental to clients if the therapists have not worked through their own sibling position issues with parents and siblings. Therapists who are not aware of these issues can be lulled into complacency or enticed into familiar fight patterns, make mistakes, or become emotionally blocked. For example, if a therapist has the same sibling position that one of the spouses in marital therapy, a symptomatic child in a family, or the parent of a client in individual therapy has, that therapist may fight battles for those family members, just as the therapist did in his or her family of origin.

Above all, therapists must remember that the systems approach to sibling positions cannot stand alone as a model or a theory for therapy. It is complementary to other models and theories. Therefore, other hypotheses that account for human behavior can be integrated with this approach. Every family is unique; only through an investigation of each particular family can therapists know whether the specific sibling positions response pattern can be helpful. Consequently, it is important for therapists to remember that sibling position response patterns are descriptive rather than predictive.

Functional and Dysfunctional Sibling Position Patterns

Although not functional or dysfunctional in themselves, sibling position patterns reflect the quality of the interaction within specific systems: individual, dyad, triad, and larger systems. There are three types of situations in which dysfunctional family patterns may occur.

1. A crisis, such as the death of a family member, loss of income, or a major failure in school, may put so much pressure on the family or on specific family members, that dysfunctional patterns develop. These new dysfunctional patterns may or may nor be permanent.

2. A family or family members often react in dysfunctional patterns when adjusting to new stages of development. Developmental changes that disruptions sometimes cause are the increasing independence of adolescents, the

addition of "our" children in a step-family, and the launching of children into school, careers, or marriage.

3. Some families and individuals exhibit chronic patterns of dysfunction.

In all three of these situations, siblings may respond to the perceived threat to them as individuals, to family members, to the marriage, or to the family unit by exaggerating or by shutting down characteristic response patterns. For example, third siblings who exaggerate their response patterns may become more introspective and unavailable than usual. First siblings have shut down when they show no interest or involvement in obtaining information about events—in other words, when they withdraw.

General Therapy Guidelines

Dysfunction can result from psychological difficulties within individuals and from problems in marital and family interaction. Sibling positions may not be related to every problem in therapy, but the following guidelines help therapists explore the possibility of such a relationship.

Family Therapy

Usually, a family seeks therapy when one of its members is having a problem that the family cannot resolve. The sibling position of the person who seems to have the problem suggests where the therapist should look in the family for dysfunctional patterns.

When the First Sibling Is Symptomatic

The therapist who treats a family with a symptomatic first sibling should examine parental expectations, rules, and values to determine if they are realistic, if the parents agree on them, and if the first sibling is consistently the standard for the family. The ways in which parents respond to the child's performance and enforce rules affect the self-esteem of the first sibling. If the parents' expectations seem overwhelming, first siblings give up and fail to achieve.

If their father is not fulfilling his role, first siblings assume responsibility for his inadequacies. First siblings fight with their father to try to make him more responsible, become overly responsible for their mother, or compensate for their father's lack of responsibility.

The therapist should also determine whether the father has any unresolved emotional "baggage" in his current family. If the father does not deal openly with his anger, for example, first siblings often act it out by being overly aggressive, being depressed, and fighting their father's battles with others. First siblings may also respond to their father's fantasies and unfulfilled dreams. These are often implicit responses, however, because the father is usually unaware of his unresolved issues. The therapist should observe to determine whether the first sibling is like the father or exactly opposite; the answer may provide some additional clues to the father's unresolved issues.

In focusing on multigenerational issues, the therapist should consider, for example, what the father learned from his father and from his father's interaction with his mother, as well as the transmission of this knowledge to the first sibling. Other dynamics to be investigated include patterns that reflect how the expectations for performance have or have not been resolved in the extended family.

When the Second Sibling Is Symptomatic

When the symptomatic family member is the second sibling the therapist should examine the incongruence in the family between implicit and explicit rules, values, and expectations. The therapist should consider mother's unexpressed conflicts with other family members, especially the father. Second siblings read the underlying structure of conflict in their parents' marriage and meld with their mother's pain about it. If they cannot resolve it, they fight their mother's battles.

In addition, the therapist should consider the mother's unresolved emotional "baggage" in the current family. Because of the melding process, second siblings usually do not know that the pain and emotional currents that they experience originate with their mother. Second siblings can be either obviously attached to their mother or appear very distant. Second sibling clients may believe that they are detached, but the underneath connections are worthy of exploration.

Second siblings can be burdened and incapacitated by such things as an incongruence, emotional currents, and unresolved conflicts from previous generations. The therapist should investigate.

When the Third Sibling Is Symptomatic

In dealing with a symptomatic third sibling the therapist first should determine whether the marital relationship has unresolved conflict at both implicit and explicit levels. When there is tension in the marriage, third siblings feel responsible for one or both parents. They may outwardly focus on the parent who seems to need the most support; behind the scenes, however, they make contact and support the other parent. If the conflict is open and the parents try to force them to take sides with one or the other, third siblings develop dysfunctional behavior patterns.

When the explicit and implicit interactional rules about such things as intimacy, fighting, decision making, expression of feelings, and affection are dysfunctional in their parents' marriage, third siblings express the dysfunction in their own behavior. For example, if decision making in the family is erratic and ineffectual, third siblings may be scatterbrained and flighty themselves. Therapists should look for patterns of unhappy marriages, mother-father-child triangles, and dyadic and triadic relationships among parents and grandparents when investigating multigenerational issues.

When the Fourth Sibling Is Symptomatic

The therapist should examine pain, conflicts, and tension in individuals and subsystems in the family when the fourth sibling is symptomatic. In addition, the therapist should examine the family's ability to work together toward a common goal. Fourth siblings assume guilt for any disruption that keeps the family from achieving its purposes.

In focusing on intergenerational issues the therapist should consider any pain or tension in individuals or relationships in the extended family that affects members of the nuclear family. Such pain can result from illness, death, divorce, disappointments, and conflictual relationships in the extended family.

Marital Therapy

If the characteristic sibling response patterns of the spouses are not exaggerated and/or shut down, the therapist can assume that the dysfunction for which a couple seeks therapy is in the interaction in the marriage. Marital problems with an interaction basis generally arise from the interface of the sibling positions and what each spouse fails to provide to the other. For instance, second siblings harass first siblings to acknowledge their implicit feelings, and first siblings see this as an invasion of privacy and a disapproving message that they are off target.

If the characteristic sibling response patterns are highly exaggerated and/or shut down in one spouse and not the other, the therapist can assume that the dysfunction is individual rather than interactional. In this situation, therapists need (1) to teach the other spouse to respond constructively to the exaggerated patterns, and (2) to provide individual therapy for the spouse with the exaggerated patterns.

If the characteristic sibling response patterns of both spouses are exaggerated and/or shut down, the therapist can assume that there are both individual and interactional reasons for the dysfunction. In this situation, the therapist should consider individual therapy for each spouse first, because the root of the dysfunction may lie within multigenerational dynamics of their families of origin. Marital therapy may be added later as indicated by the needs of each spouse and family dynamics.

Individual Therapy

Therapists should use their knowledge of characteristic sibling response patterns to help clients understand their family roles, perceptual orientation, and identity issues. Dysfunctional patterns in adults are often related to their relationships with their mother, father, and siblings. Therapists need to connect interpersonal and social relationship patterns to their relationships in their family of origin, because many individual clients present problems related to social interaction, such as failure at work, an inability to develop intimate relationships, and feelings of inferiority. An awareness of the ways in which the sibling response patterns of family members interact to maintain and aggravate such problems is extremely helpful to the therapist.

Specific Therapy Guidelines

The following guidelines outline not only specific suggestions for working with clients of each sibling position, but also the ways in which therapists' sibling positions may affect their responses to clients.

Working with First Siblings

- Release first siblings from being overly responsible to and for others.
- Validate their right to be who they are and reassure them, whenever possible, that they are on target.
- Give them a great deal of information and help their spouse and others in the family system understand the relevancy of this for first siblings.
- Use their cognitive structure to connect them to their emotions, and legitimize the emotions by making them part of relevant information.
- Provide explanations when appropriate.
- Ask direct questions and give specific answers.
- Learn when to be soft and when to be tough with first siblings.
- Understand that their resistance to role play (and to the therapist) comes from the fear of doing something wrong.

- Teach them about the relevance of their connection to their parents and their tendencies to be overly responsible for siblings and parents.
- Teach them how to be close and at the same time responsible.

If therapists working with first siblings are also first siblings, they may

- engage in power struggles with their clients, as first siblings have a need to be right;
- use explicit details inappropriately in discussions, focusing on semantics, play on words, elaboration of facts;
- become immovable and distant in response to the client's defenses and games;
- feel overwhelmed about their own and the client's expectations for positive results in therapy;
- fail to see the significance of the client's need to have feelings connected to specific incidents to establish them as legitimate.

If therapists working with a first sibling are second siblings, they may

- not provide enough explicit information, erroneously assuming that their first sibling client knows explicitly what they themselves know implicitly;
- focus on process more than outcome and on affect more than cognition, thereby glossing over the importance of results and rationality to the first sibling clients;
- polarize and deal with only one side of an issue.

If therapists working with first siblings are third siblings, they may

- focus on issues to the point that they miss details important to first sibling clients;
- disappear into introspection, and fail to provide information to the client, thus confusing the first sibling client;
- allow their tentativeness and preference for ambiguity (as third siblings) to threaten the first sibling client.

If therapists working with first siblings are fourth siblings, they may

- focus on the whole when the first sibling client is focused on the parts;
- become impatient and bored with the amount of detailed information given by the client;

- try to take care of the client's pain, but feel guilty and inadequate when the client does not permit it.

Working with Second Siblings

- Help those within the family system to assure second siblings that they have significant places in the family.
- Help second siblings separate their emotions from those of the people around them (the melding process in reverse). Connect their pain to someone else's as rapidly as possible. Teach them about boundaries and how to be separate, yet close. Give them the choice of being close to the therapist or to their siblings but, for the time being, not to their parents. Remind them to breathe, because second siblings literally hold their breath in the presence of pain. Help them experience their own pain and believe that they can deal with it.
- Help them deal with the "in betweens" instead of only "extremes," digging deeply to be aware of all the multiple levels of needs and discrepancies. Include in this process information about the world they live in, as they act on the faulty assumption that the world is the way they see it.
- Use imagery experiences and information. Ask questions on two levels, pictorial and content.
- Ask what they do not know rather than overwhelm them with unsolicited information. Do not give them explanations. Ask them what they are doing, thinking, and sensing.
- Be aware of the constant switching back and forth of polarities, and stay with the swings.
- Affirm and accept; do not reassure second siblings.
- Teach them about their connection to their parents, particularly their mother, and the significance of exaggerated patterns in relationship to their parents.

If therapists working with a second sibling are first siblings, they may

- focus on the explicit and miss the implicit to which the second sibling client responds;
- misread and mislabel the polarizations;
- become impatient with the implicit assumptions and mind reading that the second sibling does.

If therapists working with a second sibling are also second siblings, they may

- perhaps not meld with their second sibling client's emotions, but be confused and distracted by them;
- misread the implicit and assume that they know instead of helping the client to be explicit;
- polarize in the opposite direction from their second sibling client.

If therapists working with a second sibling are third siblings, they may

- focus on issues to the exclusion of underlying affect important to second sibling clients;
- become confused by the extremes that appear to have no connections and, in the eyes of the therapist, reduce the second sibling client's choices;
- confuse the client with in-and-out messages that are implicit and can be misread by the client.

If therapists working with second siblings are fourth siblings, they may

- become overwhelmed by the amount and intensity of the feelings carried by the client even though they know these feelings are the client's;
- be overwhelmed because the problems and the feelings presented by the second sibling look and feel like too much to sort out;
- fail to focus on parts of the presented problem while focusing on the Gestalt.

Working With Third Siblings

- Focus on the meanings of the third sibling's in-and-out feelings and behavior, and reframe them in a logical, acceptable manner.
- Offer them choices, help them see their choices, and help family members generate choices for them in a legitimate way.
- Restructure interaction so that they recognize choices that they do not see or that they deny.
- Give them permission to be "out" of therapy for a short period of time so that they can sort out the issues.
- Provide a connection, and let third sibling clients know that the therapist will continue to be available even though they go away at times. Stay connected even though they seem uninterested.
- Teach them the importance of the details that they often omit.

- Teach third siblings about their connection to both parents and the emphasis on the marital relationship rules. Help them examine their relationships with their parents, and help them disconnect in healthy ways.
- Help them see the relevance of their feelings, and connect them in given contexts.
- Look to the other side of what a third presents in therapy. For example, if they present information about father, ask about mother; if they say they are happy with school, ask about what at school does not please them.
- Teach them about their ambivalences, need for choices, their behavior, and this behavior's influence on others.

If therapists working with third siblings are first siblings, they may

- take away the client's choices by inferring that there is one right way or by forcing the client to make a decision;
- focus on the details of the parts of a problem to the exclusion of the connections and/or the issues on which the third sibling client may be focused;
- collude with the client to overlook the importance of feelings in certain contexts.

If therapists working with a third sibling are second siblings, they may

- inappropriately force the client to process a relationship when they are not ready to do so; this makes them feel as though they have no choice in the matter;
- focus on personal or interpersonal process when the client is focused on issues and connections between parts of experiences;
- polarize affectively and confuse the client.

If therapists working with a third sibling are also third siblings, they may

- ignore detail important to the problem, and focus on connections and context;
- inappropriately move in-and-out when the third sibling client is also moving in-and-out, or allow the client to move in-and-out without comment;
- collude with the client to dismiss relevant affect.

If therapists working with a third sibling client are fourth siblings, they may

- be paralyzed by client's pain;
- try to "fix" the system without enough focus on the connections;
- feel responsible and stymied when the third sibling client goes away.

Working With Fourth Siblings

- Help fourth siblings break the whole into parts when they are overwhelmed and feeling helpless.
- Give clear directives.
- Work to help the spouse and other family members acknowledge their own emotions and behaviors, as well as to be explicitly responsible for their parts in things that go wrong, when fourth siblings are feeling to blame.
- Be alert to people and parts of their lives that fourth siblings may have cut out because everything became too much.
- Link their flighty, unreasonable behavior to the pain they feel.
- Teach them about their sibling position role responsibilities to the family, their "garbage collecting" tendency, and their occasional helpless reaction to the pain in the family. Help them disconnect in healthy ways.
- Examine their resistance to greater awareness. Give them bits and pieces of information, and teach them that it is possible to add to the Gestalt without being totally overwhelmed.
- Make events in their lives explicit in holistic ways. Help them terminate issues and relationships. Teach them to develop personal goals.
- Do not justify, nor allow others to justify, behavior and requests to fourth siblings.
- Ask them to comment on what happens in the system.

If therapists working with a fourth sibling are first siblings, they may

- overwhelm the client with detail and explanation and fail to connect the beginning, middle, and end;
- ask too many questions in succession, or give too many directions at once;
- feel responsible for the helplessness expressed or demonstrated by the fourth sibling client.

If therapists working with a fourth sibling are second siblings, they may

- confuse their own feelings with the client's feelings;
- polarize and become analytical rather than staying with the experience;
- appear unconcerned to protect themselves from the pain of the client, or become so involved with that pain that they ignore cognitions.

If therapists working with a fourth sibling are third siblings, they may

- be inconsistent in emotional closeness to the client;
- be too cognitive and issue oriented;
- not give enough detail to break the whole into parts for the client, but rather focus on the connections.

If therapists working with a fourth sibling are also fourth siblings, they may

- become immobilized by the amount and intensity of the feelings carried by the fourth sibling client;
- feel to blame when trying to "fix" the family system for the client;
- have difficulty breaking the whole into parts.

CHAPTER *13*

Individual Therapy

Craig, a 30-year-old single man, entered therapy because he was depressed. Perceived by his colleagues and superiors at work as very productive, innovative, and progressive, he had moved up through the ranks of a reputable computer company quite rapidly to an executive position. He reported that his relationships at work were congenial and businesslike, but that he had no friends outside the work setting. He felt highly anxious in social settings of all kinds. He wanted to get married, but had been unable to establish significant relationships with women.

Craig, a first child, was seen for several months, usually once a week, but occasionally twice a week. His therapist, Dr. Adams, a forty-five-year-old man, was a first sibling. In this description of Craig's therapy, the therapist's use of sibling position information to determine issues and therapeutic strategies is emphasized.

Beginning Phase of Therapy

Establishing a therapeutic relationship and gathering information were the primary therapeutic tasks for the beginning phase of therapy, which included five sessions over three weeks. As he gathered information from Craig,

---

Note: The names of families and family members in the following case were changed to protect their true identities. As we changed identifying facts and contexts, the case became an amalgamation of many clients and family situations.

179

Dr. Adams took into account the sibling positions of Craig, his parents, his siblings, and his extended family.

Establishing a Therapeutic Relationship

Dr. Adams began to develop a therapeutic relationship with Craig during the information gathering process. Initially, Craig was defensive and guarded. He seemed to worry a great deal about whether the therapist would reveal information about him to anyone else. Craig certainly did not want others to know that he was in therapy or the reason for it. He feared others would judge him and not approve of him. Craig responded to Dr. Adams' explanations, attempts to validate Craig, and questions with rather belligerent questioning of his own, such as "What do you mean by that?" His other major responses were long periods of silence.

Recognizing that first siblings need approval and fear that they will not be "good enough," the therapist responded by giving Craig messages that his repeated questioning was "on target." Although Craig's constant questioning was really a defense, the therapist used it as an opportunity to validate Craig's feelings. Then Dr. Adams offered him information and explanations about the meaning of his questions and behaviors. Thus, the therapist first gave Craig approval for questioning and then, by taking Craig's question literally, the therapist bypassed Craig's defenses and gave him important information.

Craig's second most frequent question was "What am I supposed to do when I come here?" Dr. Adams perceived this as an attempt by a first sibling to make the structure of therapy explicit. He also recognized that Craig might be attempting to determine the authority figure's (therapist's) expectations. In this case, the therapist responded by giving explicit information about the length of therapy sessions, some of the possible outcomes, and other issues Craig might want to raise in therapy. In addition, Dr. Adams asked Craig what he wanted from therapy and what he expected from the therapist. By emphasizing the importance of Craig's input in therapy, Dr. Adams facilitated a different kind of interaction for Craig with an authority figure.

The therapist worked diligently to give Craig as much approval as possible in order to build a relationship of trust. Whenever Craig talked about any personal information, Dr. Adams thanked him for sharing these things and applauded his courage in doing so. As the relationship between Craig and his therapist solidified over the sessions, the need for constant expressions of approval decreased.

Gathering Information

One of the things Dr. Adams had Craig do in the beginning period of therapy was construct a genogram of his family of origin (see Figure 13–1). Because his family was a thousand miles away and Craig did not want them to know he was in therapy, all of the information in the genogram was filtered through his perceptions.

Craig's parents had been married for 33 years and had what Craig described as a "civil marriage," meaning that they were very proper and civil to each other. They seemed to have few explicit disagreements, although Craig thought that they disagreed on many things. He described his mother, Betty (a first child), as a hard worker who stayed at home and placed a great emphasis on the house and everything in it being clean and orderly.

During his childhood and adolescence, his mother had constantly demanded to know where he had been, whom he had been with, and what they had done. His response to this questioning was to become more and more secretive and defensive, even though he rarely had anything to hide. On the other hand, Craig felt very responsible for his mother. To gain her approval, he often lied about where he had been, whom he had been with, and what he had done. Even when he lived a thousand miles from home, he expressed concern for her. He was annoyed, however, by her frequent telephone calls to find out if he was dating someone he might marry.

Craig was protective of his father, Allen (a third child). Even though he was angry with his father for often being away from home and for not protecting him from the incessant questioning of his mother, he defended his father's need to be at work. After all, Allen was a very successful businessman and took care of the family very comfortably. Craig attributed his own acumen in the business world to his father's examples. Whenever Allen saw Craig or called him, he coached Craig on ways to impress his boss and progress in his job. Although Craig appreciated his father's interest, he was always highly anxious during and after those conversations. Craig's mixed feelings and thoughts about his parents were confusing to him.

Based on Craig's description of his parents, Allen appeared to be responsible for productivity in the family. Allen earned the money, set high expectations for the educational achievement of family members, and established a standard of living for the entire family. Therefore, the therapist assumed that Craig, being a first child, was somehow connected to the unresolved issues of his father. The therapist also assumed that Craig's anxiety was associated with his mother's critical, incessant involvement with him, as well as with his father's pressure for continued success in the business world.

Because Craig was unable to form intimate relationships with women, Dr. Adams was curious about the dynamics and quality of the marital relationship

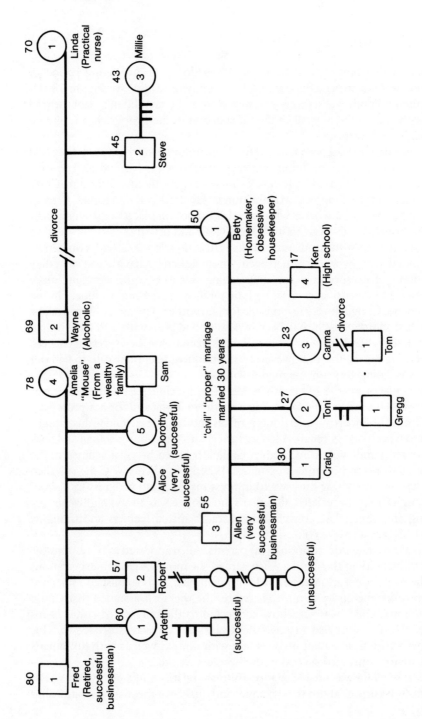

Figure 13–1 Craig's family genogram.

of Craig's parents. Knowing that first children learn about intimacy through their father's relationship to their mother and through their own relationship with their father, Dr. Adams wondered why Craig's father had not taught Craig how to establish an intimate relationship with a woman. Although he did not ask Craig to do it right away, the therapist decided that Craig needed to talk with his father about developing relationships with women.

Craig had two sisters: Toni, 27 years old, and Carma, 23 years old. Toni was married and had two sons, and Carma was divorced after a brief marriage. Both sisters did well in school, were very involved in clubs and activities, and according to Craig, they made friends easily. Craig had often fought with Toni when they both lived at home, but he had been largely disengaged from her in the last seven or eight years. She was the opposite of her mother; she was happy-go-lucky, loving, slightly irresponsible and unpredictable, and very active. Yet, she seemed to be frightened often. Craig described Carma as very attractive, rather shy, and very proper. He knew only what his mother had told him about her divorce. He attributed his lack of knowledge about her to the fact that she was seven years younger than he.

Craig also had a 17-year-old brother, Ken, who was in high school and lived at home. Craig said he did not know Ken too well either. When Ken was young and Craig lived at home, he tried to do the things with Ken that he had wanted his father to do with him. Craig was a little jealous of Ken, because Ken had a better relationship with their father than he did. He described Ken as happy, highly involved in sports and social activities, seldom at home, but a "good kid." The therapist drew no immediate assumptions from Craig's sibling relationships.

Next Dr. Adams examined Craig's connections to his grandparents. Betty's parents had been divorced when she was 10 years old, and Craig had never met her father. Craig's grandmother and his mother described his grandfather as a "drinker," someone who would rather fish or party than do an "honest day of work." According to them, Craig's grandfather never held a job long and did not provide adequately for the family. Craig heard his mother speak kindly of her father only once. She said that she cried and cried when he left because he was always affectionate, loving, and kind to her and her brother. They never heard from him again after he left. "Drunk and in some ditch," Craig's grandmother always said.

Grandmother Linda, as Craig called her, had worked as a practical nurse some of the time before his grandfather left, and all of the time after he left. Money was always very scarce. This meant that Betty, at 11 years of age, was responsible for cleaning the house, fixing some of the meals, and caring for her younger brother, Steve. Betty described her brother as likable, but somewhat lazy like their father. Craig was a little confused about that because Uncle Steve had graduated from college and was a high school teacher. He and his family used to visit Craig's family, and they all seemed noisy, busy, and happy. At each visit, Betty reminded Steve that if he had just stayed in school a little longer, he could have made more of himself. Gradually Steve and his family visited less and less.

Grandmother Linda was 70 years old, retired, and living in her own apartment not far from the family home. She and Craig's mother talked every day. Grandmother Linda told Betty that she sure was a whiner and complainer, and that she did not know why she did not "button up her lip and stiffen up her arches and get moving." She also periodically wondered out loud why Betty's family continued to put up with her.

The therapist concluded that, as a child, Betty received many messages from her mother that indicated that it was necessary for her to grow up fast. It appeared that Betty had been a surrogate mother to Steve and a confidante to her mother. Hierarchical boundaries were blurred as Betty in many ways took the place of her father. Thus, Betty had never clearly occupied the role of a child in the family, and now she and her mother were more like sisters, with Betty the older sister.

Craig always smiled when he talked about his fathers's mother, Amelia. No one in the family called her Amelia, because her husband, Fred, had christened her "Mouse" as an endearment. She did not look mousy; rather, she was pretty and entertained "correctly" with the manners and behaviors that reflected her wealthy, high-society family. She demanded and fussed at Fred in a "squeaky" manner and voice, however, about a variety of things that displeased her. Fred pampered and protected Amelia. In return, "Mouse" doted on Fred and babied him in every way possible. From Craig's perspective, they loved each other and their grandchildren, and he was never bored when he was with them.

Craig expressed some concern that his grandfather was always fussing about something that his father was or was not doing. Allen complained that his father was rigid, demanding, and confident that he knew the only correct way to do things. His first job had been for his father; although he learned a great deal, he found a job with someone else at the first opportunity.

Now that Fred was retired, he gave Allen unsolicited free advice about preparation for retirement and the management of his retirement investments. As the years progressed, Craig's father became as unavailable to his father, Fred, as he was to his own family.

Craig reported that his father's brother and sisters were all well educated, but that some of them seemed to have problems. Ardeth, the oldest, was married, had two children, and seemed to be all right. Robert, the second child, did not please his parents at all. He had been married three times, each time to an educated, successful woman. Craig knew that Uncle Robert had children from each marriage, but he did not know how many. It was common family talk that Robert had been too young when he married the first time and that he had married only because his girlfriend was pregnant. Craig thought that Uncle Robert's second wife drank too much and embarrassed the family. He was not sure what Uncle Robert did for a living because he changed jobs often.

Alice, the fourth in the family, was a very successful businesswoman who had never married and rarely contacted the family. If there was a family event, such as a wedding, a funeral, or summer outing, to which they were all invited, however, Aunt Alice always came. She intrigued Craig, but he did not know why. It may have been because, when he was young, his parents stopped talking about her as soon as he came into the room. Nothing is more frustrating to a first child than to have information denied to him.

Dorothy, the fifth sibling, married a physician while she was in college and moved to another state. Craig did not remember much about her and her family. She had six children; as he recalled, something with the children always prevented Dorothy and her family from visiting her family of origin.

In examining Allen's family, Dr. Adams identified a number of themes worthy of investigation. Allen's father was a first sibling who not only emphasized education and success in the world, but also needed to be right about everything. Robert had failed in Fred's eyes, so Fred devoted his attention to Allen to ensure that he would be successful. This kind of attention reduced Allen's choices, and he learned early to be "out" more than "in" with his father. This behavior generalized to his own family later. Although the marriage of Allen's parents was not explicitly conflictual, the rules for intimacy and negotiation were not clear. It seemed to Dr. Adams that Allen and Betty had replicated this marriage by developing a "proper" and "civil" relationship. Because Craig was having problems with intimacy in his relationships, Dr. Adams concluded that Allen had not learned from his parents' marriage how to be truly intimate and still carried this as an unresolved issue. This further confirmed Dr. Adam's theory that Craig needed to talk to his father about intimacy.

Dr. Adams also made some assumptions in regard to Craig's need for approval. Craig's grandfather, Fred, and his mother, Betty, were both highly critical of Craig's performance in everything. From his father's side of the family Craig received messages about the importance of success in work. Fred coached Allen in the management of retirement funds, and Allen in turn coached Craig in the best ways to move up in his company. Allen seemed to be duplicating with Craig the type of relationship he had with his father, except that Allen was not as critical. It was clear that Craig received approval on the basis of how he performed at work, and not on the basis of who he was.

The messages from his mother's side of the family were slightly different, but they were again related to approval. Dr. Adams hypothesized that Craig had learned from his mother's side of the family that unsuccessful men were cut off from the family. Craig had heard his mother say many times, "If husbands don't take care of their families, they should be booted out just like my father." As Craig perceived the situation, only men who did not do what women expected received disapproval. Yet, it seemed impossible to please women, since Craig could never please his mother.

Middle Phase of Therapy

During the middle phase of therapy, which consisted of 20 sessions in 10 weeks, Dr. Adams continued to gather information and test his assumptions. He developed therapeutic strategies based on his interpretations of the sibling position patterns of interaction in Craig's family.

Content Strategies

1. *Help Craig link his behaviors, feelings, and attitudes to some of the themes and issues in his extended family.*

Dr. Adams believed that if he helped Craig examine the relationships in his extended family, Craig would eventually see a connection between these relationships and his depression and anxiety. His knowledge of the impact of sibling positions helped Dr. Adams understand which relationships were important in the development of Craig's symptoms. Therefore, he concentrated his information gathering strategies around those relationships and in therapy helped Craig trace the issues in those relationships back through the extended family.

2. *Explore Craig's intimacy attempts in more depth.*

Because Craig complained that he had no friends and was unable to relate to women, and because first children learn to be intimate through their father's relationship with their mother and through their own relationship with their father, Dr. Adams asked questions about intimacy in these two relationships. As a result of this questioning, Craig acknowledged he felt anger toward his father because his father had not been very affectionate; was rarely available for wrestling, for talk, or for activities; did not share any of his feelings; and did not explore Craig's feelings with him. He felt sorry for his mother and began to understand why he felt so responsible for her. He realized that his father had not been available for her either. He asked Dr. Adams if the civility of their marriage covered the emptiness that he suspected in their relationship.

In the investigation of intimacy issues, Craig was asked to share with Dr. Adams details about every relationship he had ever had with girls and women. This was a difficult part of therapy for Craig, who kept asking questions such as "Why do you want to know about that?" and "What do you mean by that?"

These continual questions evoked a first sibling response in Dr. Adams. He became defensive because he perceived Craig's continual questions as criticism of his performance as a therapist. Dr. Adams' questioning became even more adamant; the more Dr. Adams pressed, the more Craig became immovable and unwilling to give any information. With therapy stalled Dr. Adams realized that he and Craig, two first siblings, were in a power struggle over who was more right. Dr. Adams simply asked Craig, "Is this how it felt with your mother?" This question stopped the power struggle and they were able to process what had happened. The struggle became an opportunity for Dr. Adams to offer more approval to Craig. He acknowledged his own part in it as a therapist and thanked Craig for staying in the fight and working it through.

As Craig became less defensive, he admitted that he was terribly afraid of asking a woman for a date, that every one of his past dates had been a failure, and that he was heavily involved in pornography. After revealing his "secret," Craig was willing to talk freely about his sexual behavior. Dr. Adams told Craig that he was proud of his admitting something that he had kept a secret for so long and thanked Craig for sharing it with him.

3. *Explore Craig's feelings and behaviors about sexuality.*

Craig had kept the information about his involvement in pornography a secret because of his fears of disapproval. Dr. Adams believed that Craig's intimacy problems and his feelings about his own sexuality were connected to his low self-esteem, his heightened fears of disapproval, and to his father's unresolved intimacy and sexual issues.

Dr. Adams linked Craig's fears to his need for approval by asking questions such as: "What do you think women expect from you?" "What would be so hard about giving that?" "What would you need to do to gain approval from women?" "What kind of advice would your mother give you about this?" "What kind of advice would your father give you about this?" "Are you willing to look at the possibility that what women and your mother would tell you if you asked them these questions may not be anything like the answers you just gave me?" Craig was uncomfortable when such questions were asked, but he was also very interested in this new perspective.

Dr. Adams was also curious about Craig's relationship with men. He asked questions such as "How do you get close to men?" "Have you ever had any sexual contact with men?" "Have you considered it?" In addition, he asked how Craig learned about sex, and what his sexual fantasies were.

Dr. Adams learned that Craig had no homosexual tendencies and really wanted to have a relationship with a woman. He was terrified that a woman would think he was inadequate; however, Craig simply did not know how to relate to women because of his inexperience and his dependence for information on pornographic sources. Pornography had heightened his physiological stimulation, but failed to provide sexual intimacy experiences or relationship skills.

4. *Require Craig to have a face-to-face interview with his father about his father's relationships with women.*

Because Craig was a first child, Dr. Adams wondered whether Craig was acting out one of his father's unresolved issues. Therefore, Dr. Adams required Craig to have a face-to-face conversation with his father, Allen, about intimate relationships with women. Craig was afraid and reluctant to tell his father that he was in therapy, but he decided that he did not want the secret of his therapy to be a barrier in the interview with his father. He said that he would tell his father during the interview. Dr. Adams coached Craig before he approached his father. He suggested that Craig be very explicit about the length of time he wanted and the place where they should meet. He was to refuse to take no for an answer. He was to tell his father that the purpose of their meeting was to help Craig understand his relationships in the family better.

With those decisions made, Dr. Adams coached Craig in the kinds of questions to ask. Craig was instructed to ask Allen about Allen's relationship with Betty, his relationship with Craig, his perception of his parents' marriage (Fred and Mouse), his relationship with his father and his mother, and his relationship with other women. Craig basically knew what to ask, because Dr. Adams had asked him the same kinds of questions.

Craig was most afraid of asking his father about his relationships with other women. Craig wanted to know if his father had experimented with sex before he was married, if he had a good sexual relationship with Betty, and if his father had been involved with pornography. He also wanted to know how his father learned to be intimate with women. Dr. Adams suggested that Craig ask explicitly if his father had had any affairs since he had been married.

When Craig returned from the interview, he was dumfounded. His father had disclosed his involvement in several extramarital affairs and had asked Craig to keep them a secret from his mother. Allen described his sexual relationship with Betty as "all right," but said that the rest of their relationship was matter-of-fact. Allen and Betty talked about his business matters quite freely; he did not share any of his deep personal feelings, however, and neither did she.

Craig had believed that he was unique in being uninformed about his parents' marriage, so he was surprised that Allen did not really know much about his parents' relationship. Allen reported that he had worried about his parents when he was a child, but as he got older, he did not think about them and was involved in other things.

5. *Link Craig's feelings about not being "good enough" to his self-esteem.*

Dr. Adams applauded Craig for bringing back all the information from his father. After they processed the information, he asked Craig if he was ready to stop taking care of his father's intimacy issues and start working on his own. Craig said he was ready, so Dr. Adams suggested that he choose one woman acquaintance and ask her to lunch.

First children are always worried about whether others will approve of what they do, about whether they will be "good enough," and Craig was no exception. Craig received approval primarily for his accomplishments at work and primarily from his father and his grandfather. Craig felt that both of these men appreciated him only for what he could do in the business world. On the other hand, his mother usually focused on what he did not do well. She always sent messages that he needed to do more. These two forces of limited approval and continuous disapproval combined to make Craig believe that he could never be good enough, especially with women.

Dr. Adams was consistent in giving approval, not only for what Craig did in therapy, but also for who Craig was as a person. He was explicit in letting Craig know how hard he thought Craig had worked, how much he had accomplished, and what he, Dr. Adams, enjoyed about his own relationship with Craig. Dr. Adams connected Craig's feelings of inadequacy to his fears about intimate relationships with women. As therapy progressed, Dr. Adams discussed Craig's changing attitudes and behaviors with women. He noted that Craig had taken several different women to lunch, had taken the same woman to lunch on several occasions, and had finally taken this woman to dinner and a concert.

6. *Increase Craig's awareness of his responses when others seem to disapprove of his actions or tell him he is wrong.*

When first children sense disapproval from others, they are often described as stony, immovable, and distant. When they appear this way, first children feel defiant, alone, and incapable. Dr. Adams saw these latter patterns in Craig's description of his relationship with his mother. First children do not realize that they appear stony and immovable to others, but they do realize that they appear distant. They also sense others as distant from them. Knowing this, Dr. Adams gave Craig explicit information about these patterns when they occurred in therapy. Initially, Dr. Adams pointed out these patterns after the fact. As Craig gained more and more awareness of himself as an acceptable person and sensed Dr. Adams' approval of him, however, the therapist confronted him at the time. Craig began to catch himself in these patterns occasionally and to laugh at them.

7. *Teach him to consider his desires as well as other people's expectations.*

First children sometimes become so involved in trying to gain approval by meeting someone else's expectations that they ignore their own needs. This was evident in Craig's relationship to women, as well as in his relationship with his father and grandfather. When Dr. Adams asked Craig if he had really wanted to do all the things he did to advance in the company, Craig replied, "Well, I did it for my father." Dr. Adams asked the question again, and he replied, "Well, I wanted to be successful." When asked the question a third time, he admitted that he had not wanted to do all those things, but the admission surprised him. He was proud of his success, but he realized that he had not considered his own desires and had just responded to others' expectations.

Dr. Adams asked Craig to examine his relationship with his mother from the same perspective. He asked Craig the question, "Are you aware of what you do to please your mother that you really don't want to do?" Craig was aware that much of the time he tried to please her. He added that his mother badgered him all the time about his friends and what he did with them, but he had never had the courage to tell her to stop. Sometimes he wanted to do what his mother expected him to do, but he did not believe that it would be good enough for her so he did not try.

In preparation for dealing with this issue, Dr. Adams required Craig to state his preferences in the therapeutic relationship. He insisted that Craig be explicit, asking questions such as "What do you think my expectations are in this situation?" "If you wanted to disregard my expectations, what might you do, and how could we negotiate the differences?" Craig's ability to state his own desires improved; Dr. Adams felt that he was ready to approach his mother and grandmother.

8. *Require Craig to interview his mother and grandmother about his grandfather, Wayne.*

The attitudes of Craig's mother and her mother about the worth of men were related to Craig's grandfather, Wayne. Dr. Adams suspected that because Betty was a first child, her obsession with rules and proper behavior was in some way related to her father, Wayne. Because Grandmother Linda also had a great deal of information about Wayne, Dr. Adams encouraged Craig to talk to both his mother and his grandmother. He coached Craig as he had coached Craig for the interview with his father, but Craig did not need as much help. He had more ideas of his own. Dr. Adams challenged him to find out all he ever wanted to know about his grandfather. Dr. Adams also thought Craig would develop a different relationship with his mother through this interview. In addition, Dr. Adams wanted Craig to determine whether his mother, Betty, really believed what she said about men.

Craig discovered in his conversations with Grandmother Linda that Wayne was really quite a nice person until he started drinking too much. She decided that she could not take care of Wayne and the two children, so she pressured him to leave. Craig learned a great deal about his grandfather and saw some photographs of him. He was surprised to learn that Wayne had been asked to leave and had not just abandoned the family.

When Craig talked to his mother, she started her incessant questioning about why he wanted to know all this, what would he do with the information, would it help him find a wife, and is this therapist really any good. Craig told her to stop giving him the third degree because he wanted their relationship to be different. He told her that they had never been able to understand each other because the questions were always in the way. Betty interrupted him, saying that they had a good relationship and her questioning proved that she really cared. They were all for his benefit. Craig never asked her about Wayne.

Craig had not been able to change his relationship with his mother as he had anticipated, but he felt good about himself. He had not responded to his mother as he had in the past. He saw her response as her problem, rather than his. He asked Dr. Adams what he could do about his mother. Dr. Adams turned it back to him, and Craig replied with a smile on his face, "If I could get her to come in here, we could probably work it out." At this point, they discussed the possibility of the whole family coming in for therapy. Dr. Adams told him it would be a good idea and suggested that he invite the family. He made it clear, however, that it would be Craig's responsibility to get them there.

Process Strategies

Dr. Adams' major process strategies included using the therapeutic relationship to affirm Craig and give him approval, linking Craig's affect to cognition, connecting pieces to gain a more holistic view of the world, giving Craig a great deal of information, and making the intimate relationship between therapist and client explicit.

Dr. Adams linked Craig's affective and cognitive processes by listening carefully and joining him wherever he was. For example, when Craig described his relationship with his mother in the first part of therapy, he did it in a very cognitive way. Assuming that Craig had unexpressed pain and anger, Dr. Adams asked him what he felt about his mother. Craig replied that he had no feelings about her. Dr. Adams then asked Craig what he thought other people would feel if they had similar kinds of problems with their mother. Craig thought for a moment and replied that they might be mad or sad. Asked if he could find any evidence of anger or sadness inside himself, Craig said, "Yes, I am really mad at her." Then Dr. Adams asked Craig if he had any ideas about the way that his anger was connected to his assessment of his mother and his behavior in her presence.

When Craig first came to therapy, his conception of his problems centered on his inadequacy as a person. He compartmentalized his life, separating such things as his successful career, his relationship with his mother, and his inability to have close relationships with women. He did not see that his family had any relevance to his problem. Dr. Adams' overall strategy was to help Craig link his behaviors, feelings, and attitudes to some of the themes and issues in his extended family by focusing on Craig's relationship with his father, his mother, his grandparents, and his siblings. The genogram was a visual representation of the connections. Therapy helped Craig link the pieces together to establish a more holistic view of his world.

Dr. Adams talked about intimacy in his relationship to Craig more toward the end of therapy than he had in the beginning. At first, the focus was on expectations and staying with whatever topics Craig identified. Their fight in the middle phase of therapy proved to Craig that Dr. Adams cared about him. Dr. Adams' request that Craig state his preferences and assume responsibility for these preferences moved them toward more equality in the relationship. In the end phase of therapy, Dr. Adams praised Craig for the kind of relationship they had, one that had lasted over a period of 30 weeks.

End Phase of Therapy

The final phase of therapy lasted three weeks and three sessions, although both Craig and Dr. Adams had realized several weeks earlier that they had accomplished Craig's goals. Part of the final three weeks focused on reviewing Craig's progress. Craig reported that he was less anxious and rarely depressed. He dated for fun rather than to please his parents. Although he was not as "smooth" as he wanted to be, he thought that his women friends enjoyed his company. One woman in particular was fun to be with, and she teased him outrageously about his fears and ineptness. He thought he had come a long way, as he accepted her teasing and gave up more and more of his fears and old beliefs.

Dr. Adams commented on Craig's ability to identify and express his feelings. Although this had not been one of Craig's explicit goals when he began therapy, he knew that his feelings were important because they were part of him. Furthermore, women seemed to like it when he shared his feelings.

Craig felt that he understood his relationship with both of his parents much better, but he still wanted to work in this area. He no longer felt totally responsible for the quality of his relationship with his mother, but he was dissatisfied with its current status. He was concerned about his father's dishonesty about the extramarital affairs. He knew that his relationship with his father had improved, but he felt sad because his father could not be very close to him. Craig asked his father, mother, and siblings to attend therapy with him, and they agreed to do so.

CHAPTER *14*

Family and Couple Therapy

Craig (see Chapter 13), his parents, and his three siblings attended two family therapy sessions. This was followed by a couple therapy session with Craig's parents.

Family Therapy

Craig's family came from several different geographical locations to attend two family therapy sessions, one that was four hours long and one that was three hours long. After the first session, Craig's parents requested a session by themselves. An outcome of that session was that the parents decided to have marital therapy after they returned home. One month later, Dr. Adams saw the parents and Craig in a follow-up session.

Preparation for Therapy

Prior to the family session, Dr. Adams and Craig identified and discussed some issues for the family therapy sessions. Craig's major goal was to find out how his siblings and his parents felt about him and to let them know that he wanted closer relationships with them. Because he believed that the members of his family had never talked to each other about these kinds of things, he was worried that someone would be hurt, angry, or sad; he knew that he had experienced all those feelings during his therapy, and anticipated that family members would also. Yet Craig wanted the family to understand him and know him for who he really was. He was frightened, because he did not really know if they would accept him.

His biggest worry involved the secret of his father's affairs. Craig wondered if anyone else in the family knew about them. He was concerned that if they were brought out into the open, his parents would get a divorce, everyone would be upset, and he would lose any chance of improving his relationship with each of his parents and his sisters and brothers. Nevertheless, he was disgusted with the dishonesty in the family, and he was acutely aware that he had kept secrets too.

Dr. Adams pointed out to Craig that there seemed to be two themes in the kinds of things he wanted from his family. The first theme dealt with relationships between him and each family member; the second, with family secrets. Craig agreed that these issues were important to him. When Craig asked what to do about the fact that his father had asked him to keep his affairs secret from the rest of the family, Dr. Adams answered that Craig could choose secrets as the theme of the first family session, with the option of focusing on other family member's secrets or his own. If he chose to confront his father about his affairs, however, most likely his father would run. Because Allen was the third sibling in his family of origin, choices were likely to be very important to him. Allen would probably view a confrontation by Craig as forcing him into "something." Craig responded that he had seen his father do the same thing in other situations. As a consequence, Craig chose to begin the session by sharing with the family his secrets and his desire to have better relationships with them.

Craig was afraid that his mother would react to him in the same old critical way. His goal was to remain open, to disclose what he wanted to disclose, and to keep from becoming stony and immovable. He asked Dr. Adams to help him do this. Dr. Adams reassured Craig that he had learned new skills in therapy that would help him be different with his mother, particularly his ability to identify and share his feelings.

Beginning of the Session

After the introductions, Dr. Adams told the family that Craig had invited all the family members because he wanted their help; that he and Craig had talked about what Craig wanted to do in the session; that his role, Dr. Adams', was to facilitate the exchange between family members; that their attendance at the session showed their investment in Craig and the family; that he and Craig were interested in each of them and wanted the family sessions to meet some of their needs, if they so chose.

Dr. Adams continued by suggesting that a discussion of explicit rules for interaction in the session often helped a session such as this one. These rules usually centered on confidentiality, disclosure, and honesty. Confidentiality is always a trust issue. In family sessions, disclosure sometimes means breaking family and relationship rules, and revealing personal and family secrets about self and others. Each of them could decide what information to reveal and how much. Honesty is a personal decision. During this time in the session, family members were very cautious, and no one wanted to talk very much or propose anything. It was evident, however, that each person had listened carefully and was thinking about what Dr. Adams had said.

Craig initiated a discussion of everyone's expectations and goals for the session by presenting his. He said that most of his expectations centered on saying what he wanted to say about himself and his feelings without being defensive or dishonest. He added that he cared about each one of them, and he wanted a closer relationship with each one of them. Most family members agreed that they had not known what to expect and that they were there to help Craig. Toni and Ken both said that Craig had changed, and they liked the change. No one commented on Craig's goals or said that they had any personal goals.

Middle of the Session

As Craig talked about his experience in therapy and his issues with the family, Dr. Adams facilitated interaction among family members, not only with Craig, but also with other family members as well.

Craig told his family what he had learned about himself as a first child. He mentioned his rigidity, his reliance on facts and cognition, his tendency to compartmentalize when he was afraid, and his need to be right and receive approval for what he did. With Dr. Adams' help, he had learned to focus on the family as a whole, and this had freed him to look at himself in new ways. He now saw how pieces of information fit together, and this helped him to see how family relationships were connected as well. During this time, the family listened, asked a few questions, and commented on things they had not known before. Toni said that she was glad that Craig was finally getting some things straightened out. Although somewhat vague and implicit, Toni's response illustrated a second child's appreciation when anyone in the family makes explicit something that has been implicit for years.

Sexuality

Craig decided to talk about the most frightening subject first. He told the family that he had been involved in pornography for several years, and he associated this with his inability to develop intimate relationships with women. Because of what he had learned in therapy, he said he was dating several women and was quite proud of what he had been able to accomplish. He told them that he no longer had the interest or the time for pornography. He also said that, in exploring this issue, he found himself to be quite naive and uninformed about sexuality and very inexperienced in establishing constructive relationships with either women or men.

At this point, Craig turned to his father and said, "When I realized this, I was really angry with you because I thought you should have taught me what I did not know." Allen was startled and replied that he did not know about Craig's problems with relationships. Knowing that the way to engage third siblings in therapy is to acknowledge their need to have choices, Dr. Adams pointed out to Allen that he could choose how to respond to his son, to the therapist, and to the rest of his family members. Dr. Adams also told Allen that he could talk to Craig either here or outside of therapy. Allen acknowledged Dr. Adams' comments, but did not engage Craig any more.

Self-Esteem Issues

At one point in the session, Craig discussed his belief that he could never do anything right and that he was unsuccessful in many areas of his life. Both Carma and Ken quickly chimed in that they could not understand how Craig could feel this way. He had been so successful in school and at work. Ken said that he had always thought that Craig could do anything. [Ken is the fourth child in this family, and his comments may be related to the fourth child's role of smoothing over other people's pain.]

Craig explained that he always tried to win the approval of everyone, especially his parents. He never seemed to be good enough for Mom, however, and Dad recognized only what he did at school and work. Craig said, "I have progressed a lot in this area and learned that who I am is a lot more important than what I do and how somebody else sees it."

Craig turned to his mother and said, "Nothing I ever did was good enough for you. You always seemed to think that I should do things different or better." Betty said that she told him many times what he did right and she did not know where he got this crazy idea. In the following minutes, Craig and his mother exchanged angry words, defending their own positions. They argued about the meaning of what they said and accused each other of distorting their words.

After a few minutes of this, Dr. Adams asked other family members if they had observed this pattern between Craig and his mother before. They had. Then he asked Craig and his mother if they wished to change this pattern; they did. Dr. Adams explained to them that first children often get caught in power struggles over who is right. He asked them to think about their behavior in the interaction over the last few minutes and answer the following questions: "Did you really mean what you said to the other person?" "What do you really want from each other?" "How do you feel when you get the kind of responses that you got?" "Do you have any idea what your responses are about?" Dr. Adams' questions were designed to get Craig and his mother to take an outsider's view of their power struggle.

In the session, they processed each of the questions, and then Dr. Adams said to Craig, "Will you tell your mother how you would like your relationship to be different?" Craig told his mother that he did not want to have to prove himself to her anymore, that he knew he had been critical of her, and that he did not want to do that anymore. He just wanted to tell her what he was really like and have her listen, and to do the same for her. As Craig was saying this, Betty had tears in her eyes; she said that she was sorry and that she wanted this too.

Dr. Adams asked Betty to consider whether her feelings behind the "third degree behavior" were all directed toward Craig or whether some of her feelings, such as anger, could possibly be directed toward her husband, her in-laws, her parents, or her other children. There was not time in this session for Betty to explore these possibilities, so Dr. Adams suggested that she could go back to the hotel and think about it. If she chose, they could discuss it in the next session.

Family Relationships

With the help of Dr. Adams, Craig planned to negotiate a closer relationship with each member of his family. Because second children are aware of the underlying tensions of their mother, Dr. Adams felt that Toni was probably upset about the interaction she had just witnessed between Craig and Betty. He chose to have Craig start his negotiations with Toni.

Dr. Adams connected Toni directly to her mother by asking "What do you usually do when your mother is upset?" and "Do you ever see yourself acting the same way as your Mom with Craig?" Toni told Dr. Adams that she always seemed to sense when her mother was upset, even though she lived 500 miles away. After she sensed this, she often received a telephone call from her mother because her mother was upset about something. Toni usually listened to her, comforted her, and tried to make "it" all right. She had never thought about her mother's interactions with Craig. When they were children at home, however, she and Craig had terrible battles, and some of their fights were just like those between Craig and their mother. [Second children often connect and meld with their mother's feelings and wishes and seem to have a special sense about their mother's feelings, even when they are not in the same room with them. Toni's care-giving for her mother is typical of second children. The pattern of Toni's fights with Craig was similar to that of her mother's fights with Craig because Toni had melded with some of her mother's issues and feelings and enacted these in her fights with Craig.]

Toni mentioned she noticed a difference in Craig when he called to ask her to come to this session. He talked about his feelings and inquired about hers in relationship to the therapy. He seemed softer, more open, and more interesting. She told Craig that she wanted to have a closer relationship with him.

Toni reported that she was often confused about her feelings for her father. Sometimes, she could be real close to him and have fun, but other times, she could not. At times, she was mad at him because he seemed angry or upset, but he would never talk about it. He told her not to worry about it, that he would take care of it, but it seemed to her that he never did anything about it. [In Toni's relationship with her father, Allen, she had difficulty understanding his in-and-out behavior. Because he is a third child, he sorts out feelings on his own and does not involve others. Being a second child, Toni tuned into the implicit messages in all three of these family relationships, although all the messages were denied at the explicit level.]

Dr. Adams turned to Carma and asked, "What have you thought about what has happened so far?" She said, "I really did not want to come. I had a lot of things to do, and this has taken four days out of my life. At first, I told Craig that I did not know whether I could make it or not. Then I got a call from Mom, and she said that the whole family was going to be there and I should be too." Dr. Adams asked, "Well now that you are here, can you see anything that you can get out of it?" [This question is an attempt to get Carma to realize that she has more choices available than being there or not being there. When she recognized that, she was more willing to interact with the other family members.]

Craig asked his brother and sisters how they viewed their parents' marriage. Dr. Adams asked Carma if she would share her views of her parents' marriage with Craig. [Up to that point in the session, Carma had appeared fairly uninvolved. She had not volunteered any information about herself or others. Third children usually know a great deal about dyadic relationships in the family, especially the marriage, but they often do not tell other people unless asked. This question was an attempt to connect Carma to the marriage and to Craig at the same time.]

Carma said that she often worried about her parents' relationship. They seemed so distant and straight. They did not fight, at least in the presence of their children, but it seemed that they should. Carma was puzzled that her father could be so involved at work that he never was available for her mother. Although her mother seemed angry most of the time, she never fought with their father, and only with her children one by one. During this exchange, the parents listened intently, but they did not look at each other.

Craig asked Carma if she was willing to have a closer relationship with him. After hesitating for a long time, Carma replied that she did not see anything wrong with their relationship. She was not sure how much time she had or what Craig really wanted. Maybe it would be "Okay" to do something to get closer, but she really could not make it a sure thing. [These kinds of responses are typical of a third child, as Carma was keeping her choices available by remaining ambivalent.]

Craig told Carma that he needed her to be more committed and more specific. As Craig became more demanding, Carma became more ambivalent. Dr. Adams interrupted and asked each of them to examine their interaction, and then asked Betty and Allen if their interaction ever resembled the one between Craig and Carma. [Craig's interaction with Carma is typical of the way in which first children's need for explicit information seems to limit choices for third children. Dr. Adams connected this pattern to the marriage of Allen and Betty, because they are first and third siblings.]

Dr. Adams processed all these interactions and helped them be explicit about what they learned. Carma realized that she was afraid to be close to men and that Craig's insistence just made it worse. Then she added that although she was frightened and did not know how to do what Craig was asking, she really wanted to have a closer relationship with Craig.

Ken had been very interested in all that had happened, and he volunteered that he wanted a closer and more meaningful relationship with Craig before Craig asked him. He told Dr. Adams that he had done a really good job with Craig and the family. He had never seen his family talk this much to each other before, and he really liked it. [Fourth children respond to pain and tensions that keep the family from achieving its purposes. Even though Ken was an active, happy high school senior, he felt the pain within the family system, especially in his parent's marriage. Ken's reaction to the therapy session was one of relief, because it seemed that everyone was agreeing to be more unified and more like a happy family. Fourth siblings, if they are not symptomatic, make excellent co-therapists, interacting with the therapist and giving additional information.]

End of the Session

The family had been together for a little over four hours, and Dr. Adams congratulated them on how hard everyone had worked. He reminded them of the meeting time for the session on the next day and told them that they were free to talk together about what had happened.

Couple Therapy

After the first family session, Betty and Allen discussed some of the things that had happened in therapy. One outcome for Betty was that she realized how angry she had been with Allen. About 12 years ago, a friend had told her about an affair that Allen was having. Although Betty was hurt, she was also afraid. She knew how much her family had suffered from the effect of a divorce, and she did not think she could handle it. She was also very concerned about appearances. Mouse and Fred had disapproved of their son's marriage to her at first, and she thought she would be blamed in some way if there was a divorce.

In the family session, she realized that divorce was not the only alternative. After hearing Craig talk about his first sibling patterns, she decided that she had been rigid and restrictive in her perception of her relationship with Allen. She was ready to look at some alternatives. She also saw that there was more support for her in the family than she had thought and, therefore, she was willing to risk divorce. So she confronted Allen about the affair and told him how angry and hurt she was.

Years ago, Allen had suspected that Betty was at least suspicious of him; he knew that their relationship had shifted in some way. He had been terrified to explore the reasons for the change, because he was afraid that she would divorce him and that his parents would disapprove. He also knew that he did not want to lose Betty and the children.

When Betty confronted Allen, he told her that she was right and expressed his regret. He had wanted to have closer personal relationships with her and the children all of their married life and did not know why he could not. He told Betty that he loved her and wanted to be more honest. Betty, who knew that she had not been honest either, wanted the same thing. During the discussion, as frightened as he was, Allen told Betty that he had had several affairs. About four o'clock in the morning, after tears and long discussions, they decided to ask Dr. Adams to see just the two of them before the next family session. Dr. Adams saw them in the morning for two hours before he met with the family at five o'clock.

Dr. Adams suspected that some of their problems centered on unresolved issues with their parents. He could share with them some of his thoughts about those issues, but as time was limited, they would have to see another therapist in the city where they lived. Dr. Adams suggested that it would be beneficial to talk about what to do with this information in the family therapy session.

During the time they had together, Dr. Adams asked Allen to discuss his parents' marriage. [Dr. Adams assumed that Allen's identity was very connected to the rules of his parents' marriage and so he asked him to start there.]

Allen was really puzzled in some ways about his parents' marriage, because they seemed to be very devoted to each other. His mother was such a flighty, impulsive, timid kind of person that he could not understand why his father ever married her. His father was so decisive and so right about everything that he did not know how his mother could stand him.

Dr. Adams asked Allen what he learned from his parents' marriage that might be connected to his affairs. [Dr. Adams assumed that Allen learned the rules for intimacy from his parents' marriage. It seemed to Dr. Adams that intimacy was always sought for in the marriage between Fred and Mouse, but it was not explicit enough for Allen to understand it. Dr. Adams wondered if Allen, failing to find intimacy in his marriage, moved from affair to affair in a search for closeness. Dr. Adams also knew that affairs represented the ultimate or extreme in a third sibling's in-and-out behavior.]

The therapist also asked Allen in what ways his relationship with Betty was like his relationship with his father, and he asked Betty in what way her relationship with Allen was opposite to her relationship with her father. [Betty is a first child and Fred is a first child. Therefore, Dr. Adams wanted Allen to look at his interaction with first siblings. Dr. Adams wondered if Betty had married Allen, who was the opposite of her father in many ways, in some attempt to compensate.]

Betty and Allen discussed the family therapy session that was going to occur later that afternoon, but they did not know whether to disclose to their children Allen's affairs and the reaction that Betty had to them. They also wondered if they should talk about their session with Dr. Adams and tell the children that they planned to go to therapy when they got home. The therapist explored with them the probable reactions of each of their children. Dr. Adams assumed that Craig would be relieved, because he did not have to keep his father's secrets any longer and because he saw both his parents doing something constructive about their marriage. Because Toni was a second child, she would be relieved by Betty's explicitness about her own pain. Carma would be relieved to have the conflict in the marriage made explicit, as it would make it possible for her to be closer to both her parents and help her to work on her relationships with men. Although Ken might initially be very upset at the disclosure, he could be reassured by the fact that Allen and Betty were committed to their marriage and receiving further therapy. Allen and Betty decided to disclose all the information in question in the family session.

Second Family Therapy

The family met in the second session and shared thoughts, feelings, old memories, love, fear, sorrow, and laughter on a far different note than in the first session. The focus was less on Craig and more on the family, with an initial emphasis on Allen and Betty, whose willingness to be honest about their relationship and to share their pain and their intentions to repair and build their relationship was very helpful to their children. In one way or another, they each made commitments to a closer, loving, fighting (if necessary) family.

Epilogue

As part of a research project on couple interaction at Brigham Young University, we have focused on comparing interaction patterns of specific marital sibling combinations. In addition to information from questionnaires, analyses of couple interaction with a 20-minute recorded video tape of the various sibling marital combinations is underway, but not complete. Two doctoral dissertations are finished, however; one that compares marriages of first and second siblings to marriages of second and third siblings (Hardman, 1984), and one that compares marriages of two first siblings to marriages of two second siblings (Dastrup, 1986). Although some of the data is relevant to the information on marital combinations, we chose not to include it because we do not have data on all combinations. Also, the descriptions of the patterns are dependent on the models of the coding schemes used in the analyses and do not embrace all that we discuss in this book. When the project is completed, all sibling marital combinations will be analyzed and the data published.

For those interested in this research we direct you to the specific dissertations. We anticipate that this book and couple interaction research will generate investigations by others and add to our understanding of how sibling position response patterns affect marital combination patterns.

REFERENCES

Dastrup, S. L. (1986). *Interaction in marital combinations of identical ordinal position dyads: Based on a systems approach to sibling positions.* Unpublished doctoral dissertation, Brigham Young University, Provo, UT.

Hardman, R. (1984). *The relationship between verbal interaction and marital combinations: Based on the systems theory of ordinal position.* Unpublished doctoral dissertation, Brigham Young University, Provo, UT.

Appendix

The tables in this appendix are summaries of the characteristic response patterns for each of the four sibling positions described in Chapters 4–7. They are useful for quick references when working with individuals, couples, and families.

Table A–1 Family role patterns for first-born siblings.

Job assignment	Interpersonal responsibilities	Social interactions
1. Responsible for supporting family rules, values, and expectations	1. Responsible for each family member to one parent, often father, but may be mother	1. Interact with individuals
2. Responsible for outcomes, results, products	2. Responsible for that same parent	2. Some performance anxiety in most relationships and social situations
3. Responsible for a central place in the family in order to be productive	3. Responsible for all family members' productivity	3. Feel impelled to respond to others' expectations
		4. Can be direct and engaged
		5. Will encourage others to express ideas and feelings if seen relevant

Table A–2 Perceptual orientation patterns for first-born siblings.

Focus/awareness	Cognitive patterns	Affective patterns
1. Focused on rule governed aspects of reality	1. Use ideas and facts in a logical and analytical manner to understand	1. Identify and label own and others' feelings easily if relevant
2. Focused on details and parts	2. Perceptually limited, lack of linkages between parts, compartmentalize	2. Integrates and shares own feelings if the purpose and outcome is made explicit
3. Aware of some of the implicit environment, but needs to be reminded to look	3. Go from parts to the whole	3. Can be lost, confused, and overwhelmed by detail
		4. Sometimes deny feelings

Table A–3 Identity/well-being patterns for first-born siblings.

Self-esteem	Threatened psychologically	Responses to threat	What they need from others
1. Self-esteem based on doing well in the eyes of others	1. By being "off target" in the eyes of others	1. Experience life as hopeless	1. Recognition and acceptance as being central, "on target," and productive
2. Need to feel productive and successful	2. When ignored by others as central	2. Withdraw, ignore	2. Approval of products
3. Need to be "on target"—right	3. Anticipation of performance evaluation	3. Appear "stoney," "black of countenance," unfeeling," "immoveable"	3. Exploration of feelings, failures, and helplessness with connections to behavior and logic in a reasonable way without discounting them
4. Need recognition of being central	4. Too many details, too many people needing assistance, too much disorganization	4. Can be dogmatic	4. Help in making rules, values, and expectations explicit
		5. Can be super-rational	5. Obedience to rules

Table A–4 Family role patterns for second-born siblings.

Job Assignment	Interpersonal responsibilities	Social interactions
1. To be perceptive and supportive to the implicit elements in family rules and relationships	1. To have a unique relationship with everyone in the family	1. Tender, sensitive, caring to individuals, or rational, distant, and goal-oriented
2. To open clogged channels of communication by making the implicit explicit	2. To be responsible for mother and to mother and father	2. Can be unaware of personal and others' boundaries
3. To monitor the quality of performance	3. Responsible for the affective state of each family member by supporting their emotional needs	
4. To act out the discrepancies between the implicit and explicit to force acknowledgement	4. Work with, fight if necessary with, first sibling. Flush out discrepancies between implicit and explicit rules	

Table A–5 Perceptual orientation patterns for second-born siblings.

Focus/awareness	Cognitive patterns	Affective patterns
1. Focused more on affect, implicit messages, and process than content	1. Perceive issues in terms of polarities with difficulty of integrating to supply the middle parts	1. Feel other people's tensions and feelings and absorbs them as if their own
2. Aware of symbolic and imaginative meaning	2. Restrict perception sometimes because of missing middle pieces	2. Sometimes can not sort out and label own feelings
3. Can be focused on the literal meaning of a phenomenon, logical and analytical, with form and structure the outcome	3. Need to know implicit and explicit to make sense of the whole	3. Can become blocked and burdened with details, parts, and emotions
4. Aware of underlying structure, often implicity	4. Create images to understand	4. Feel as well as thinks in polarities (mood swings)
	5. Use underlying structure to complete whole	

Table A–6 Identity/well-being patterns for second-born siblings.

Self-esteem	Threatened psychologically	Responses to threat	What they need from others
1. Identity derived from filling emotional gaps or being in touch with underlying structure in a situation	1. Loss of unique acknowledged place	1. Feel wiped out	1. Acceptance as a person with a place, clear boundaries
2. Based on having well defined boundaries in a unique place	2. Incongruencies between implicit and explicit rules, feelings, values, expectations	2. Polarize to intellect and tasks	2. To have people own their own feelings and expectations by making them explicit
3. Clearing discrepancies between implicit and explicit rules, values, feelings, and expectations	3. Other people's emotional overloads	3. Polarize to emotional and act irrationally and irresponsibly	3. To receive feedback from others if they are taking on others' feelings with reminders to let go
4. Self-sufficient and purposeful		4. Appear remote, uninvolved, overly involved, helpless, aimless	
		5. Look stubborn	

Table A–7 Family role patterns for third-born siblings.

Job assignment	Interpersonal responsibilities	Social interactions
1. Responsible for the dynamics and quality of marital relationships	1. To be connected to both mom and dad	1. Negotiate, balance
2. Responsible for the balance in all dyadic relationships	2. To restore balance in the marital relationship by connecting with each parent	2. Want to remain detached, but connected, so can appear "tentative" — one foot in, one foot out
3. To discover and enforce rules about the degree and nature of relationship rules such as closeness, conflict, dependency, intrusiveness, and loyalty	3. Responsible for connecting to all dyadic relationships in the family	3. Difficulty making a commitment to a relationship, but once committed, very difficult to get out
4. To identify family issues		4. "In and out." Fully there one moment, gone the next—psychologically or physically

Table A–8 Perceptual orientation patterns for third-born siblings.

Focus/awareness	Cognitive patterns	Affective patterns
1. Aware of connections and correlations, but not always consciously	1. To derive meanings, looks at connections, correlations, issues, and context	1. Sometimes look unfeeling
2. Focused on issues and relationships in the context	2. Uses connections to get bigger parts to get to the whole	2. Feel deeply and can identify and share feelings if they are connected to the context
3. Focused on feelings and ideas of people as connections to parts and relationships	3. Because of lack of information about details and facts may limit the context prematurely	3. To be relevant, feelings have to be clearly part of a context
	4. Rearrange and synthesize existing ideas into new forms rather than seeking meaning of separate parts	

Table A–9 Identity/well-being patterns for third-born siblings.

Self-esteem	Threatened psychologically	Responses to threat	What they need from others
1. Self-esteem is connected to the stability of the marital relationship	1. Lack of choices	1. Feel confined and trapped if they do not perceive choices	1. Appreciation for what they do
	2. Discrepant ideas, feelings		2. Recognition that they care
2. Self-esteem is tied to their ability to discover dyadic relationship rules and apply them in maintaining balance	3. Interpersonal conflict, self and others	2. Uncaring, apathetic, ambivalent, carefree	3. Help in creating choices when stuck
	4. When they perceive they have to make decisions affecting the welfare of others	3. Disappear into introspection	4. Recognition of their need for choices
		4. Turn off feelings and withdraw	5. Acceptance of their in-and-out behavior
		5. Inundated and chaotic	6. Confirmation that they can come back, that they have an enduring connection
		6. Stuck, stubborn	

Table A–10 Family role patterns for fourth-born siblings.

Job assignment	Interpersonal responsibilities	Social interactions
1. Responsible for family unity and harmony	1. Connects to each family member to assure unity and harmony	1. Develop pleasant relationships in functional families
2. Responsible for family purposes and goals	2. Responsible for all "garbage" in the family because it disrupts unity and harmony	2. Feel blamed and burdened by anything "wrong" in relationships of family
	3. Act out the tensions in relationships; can be quite dramatic	3. Make relationships easily, although sometimes superficially
		4. Impulsive and highly demonstrative with warmth and closeness expressed openly

Table A–11 Perceptual orientation patterns for fourth-born siblings.

Focus/awareness	Cognitive patterns	Affective patterns
1. Focused on the whole field (Gestalt)	1. Thinks in terms of total systems, conclusions, and outcomes	1. Can be overwhelmed by the size of the "whole"
2. Focused on purposes and goals of the system	2. Look first at the whole and then the parts	2. In touch with feelings of selves and others
3. Aware of power and responsibility	3. Leave out or does not see details, and summarize superficially, prematurely, and dramatically	3. Impulsive and demonstrative
	4. New information accepted only if it can be integrated into the whole	4. Collect negative feelings of others as burdens, but do not confuse them with their own

Table A–12 Identity/well-being patterns for fourth-born siblings.

Self-esteem	Threatened psychologically	Responses to threat	What they need from others
1. Tied to being part of the family and having purposes and goals clear and moving	1. Perception of the size of the whole	1. Overwhelmed by size of the whole so will cut out parts and people until they can manage it (unconsciously)	1. To be told that they are not blamed for pain and tension in the family or relationships
2. Well-being high when unity and harmony in the family experienced	2. Disruptive pain in family or relationships	2. Irresponsible and helpless, random ineffective behaviors	2. Help in assuming their part in conflict so that they do not assume the whole burden
3. Can have secure sense of self and see themselves as limited in their ability to change things	3. Too much pain in the family	3. "Cute," "babyish" in acting out	3. Lots of approval
	4. Sense of being blamed by family for pain	4. Stubborn layers of protection	4. For people to own their own feelings and responsibilities

Table A–13 Comparison of sibling position patterns.

Sibling variables	Sibling positions			
	First	*Second*	*Third*	*Fourth*
Role demands	Results	Quality of performance	Maintenance of balance	Maintenance of harmony and unity
Serve the system	Overt demands for productivity	Affective status of individuals	Quality of relationships between family members	Relationships as selected in the entire system
Appearance to others	Responsible, distant	Polarized, close or distant	Ambivalent, close or distant	Purposeful, close
Interpersonal responsibilities	To one person at a time	To one person at a time	To dyads	To the family system
Perceptual orientation	Analytical, rational, parts and details	Analytical, affective, parts and details	Syndetic, how parts fit together	Syndetic, Gestalt, beginning, middle and end
Identity issues	To be on target	To have a place	To have choices	To have harmony

Index

guidelines for parenting, 151–53,
155–56
guidelines for therapy and, 170–71,
173, 175–77, 178
and identity and sense of well-being,
64–67, 211
intimacy and, 111–12
fourth adolescent siblings and,
115
loyalty and, 158–59
marital dyad analysis
married to first siblings, 93–95
married to fourth siblings, 90–93
married to second siblings, 86–90
married to third siblings, 104–105
as perceptual orientation, 210
affective patterns and, 64

awareness and, 63
cognitive patterns and, 63–64
Trust in personal relationships, third
child and, 62
Twins, 136, 163
sibling position patterns and, 29–30

U

Underachievers, first children as, 36

W

Well-being. *See* Sense of well-being
Withdrawal, first child and, 44